WORLD RELIGIONS
HINDUISM
FOURTH EDITION

WORLD RELIGIONS

African Traditional Religion
Baha'i Faith
Buddhism
Catholicism & Orthodox Christianity
Confucianism
Daoism
Hinduism
Islam
Judaism
Native American Religions
Protestantism
Shinto
Sikhism
Zoroastrianism

WORLD RELIGIONS
HINDUISM
FOURTH EDITION

by
Madhu Bazaz Wangu
Series Editors: Joanne O'Brien and Martin Palmer

CHELSEA HOUSE
PUBLISHERS
An imprint of Infobase Publishing

Hinduism, Fourth Edition

Chelsea House
An imprint of Infobase Publishing
132 West 31st Street
New York NY 10001

Library of Congress Cataloging-in-Publication Data
Wangu, Madhu Bazaz.
 Hinduism / by Madhu Bazaz Wangu. — 4th ed.
   p. cm. — (World religions)
 Previously published: 3rd ed. New York : Facts on File, 2006.
 Includes bibliographical references and index.
 ISBN 978-1-60413-108-6 (alk. paper)
 1. Hinduism—Juvenile literature. I. Title. II. Series.

 BL1203.W35 2009
 294.5—dc22

         2008043047

Chelsea House books are available at special discounts when purchased in bulk quantities for businesses, associations, institutions, or sales promotions. Please call our Special Sales Department in New York at (212) 967-8800 or (800) 322-8755.

You can find Chelsea House on the World Wide Web at http://www.chelseahouse.com

This book was produced for Chelsea House by Bender Richardson White, Uxbridge, U.K.
Project Editor: Lionel Bender
Text Editor: Ronne Randall
Designer: Ben White
Picture Researchers: Joanne O'Brien and Kim Richardson
Maps and symbols: Stefan Chabluk
Cover printed by Creative Printing
Book printed and bound by Creative Printing
Date printed: November 2010
Printed in China

10 9 8 7 6 5 4 3 2

This book is printed on acid-free paper.

All links and Web addresses were checked and verified to be correct at the time of publication. Because of the dynamic nature of the Web, some addresses and links may have changed since publication and may no longer be valid.

CONTENTS

PREFACE

Almost from the start of civilization, more than 10,000 years ago, religion has shaped human history. Today more than half the world's population practice a major religion or indigenous spiritual tradition. In many 21st-century societies, including the United States, religion still shapes people's lives and plays a key role in politics and culture. And in societies throughout the world increasing ethnic and cultural diversity has led to a variety of religions being practiced side by side. This makes it vital that we understand as much as we can about the world's religions.

The World Religions series, of which this book is a part, sets out to achieve this aim. It is written and designed to appeal to both students and general readers. The books offer clear, accessible overviews of the major religious traditions and institutions of our time. Each volume in the series describes where a particular religion is practiced, its origins and history, its central beliefs and important rituals, and its contributions to world civilization. Carefully chosen photographs complement the text, and sidebars, a map, fact file, glossary, bibliography, and index are included to help readers gain a more complete understanding of the subject at hand.

These books will help clarify what religion is all about and reveal both the similarities and differences in the great spiritual traditions practiced around the world today.

Current Hindu Population

80% and over

12%–80%

2%–11.9%

0%–1.9%

© Infobase Publishing

CHAPTER 1

INTRODUCTION: THE MODERN HINDU WORLD

Hinduism is one of the oldest religions in existence. After Christianity and Islam it ranks as the world's third-largest religion. Today there are more than 950 million Hindus worldwide.

The majority of Hindus live in India, where the religion was born, and where they are over 80 percent of the population. The only officially Hindu country, Nepal, also has the highest Hindu population rate, at 89 percent. There are significant Hindu minorities in Bangladesh and Indonesia, and smaller groups can be found in Sri Lanka, Pakistan, Fiji, Guyana, Africa, Great Britain, Canada, and the United States. While Hindus in each of these societies have altered their religion to suit the needs of their cultures, all Hindus share a core of rich, poetic, and complex traditions.

Unlike Buddhism, Confucianism, Daoism, Christianity, Islam, or many of the other active world religions, Hinduism was not founded by one individual. Rather it is the result of many religious beliefs and philosophical schools coming together. The different schools of thought and doctrines that flourished on Indian

Hindu women bathe in the waters of the sacred river Ganges at Varanasi in northern India. The river is a source of life and energy.

Ornate sculptures of deities cover the tower of a south Indian temple. The stories of gods, their power, and their roles are found in a variety of written and oral sources from different periods in the history of India.

soil over the centuries were not originally labeled as *Hindu*. Nor was there a religion called *Hinduism*. *Hindu* is the Persian name for the river Sindhu, in what is now Pakistan. Thus, the people who lived near the Sindhu River came to be called *Hindus*.

In later centuries Arabs, Turks, Afghans, and Mughals—which are all Muslim groups—used the term *Hindu* to describe those in India who did not believe in Islam. It is important to note that

not all of those who were grouped together as Hindus at the time were followers of Hinduism.

Early Hinduism combined the religions of the Indus Valley in northwestern India with that of Aryan migrants from Persia. Later, Hinduism developed a more solid foundation through the writings and interpretations of the great Hindu scriptures. Throughout its many years Hinduism has been influenced by the challenges of foreigners. India found itself conquered and ruled repeatedly by foreign invaders—Greeks, Scythians, Turks, Afghans, Mughals, and the British. The unique cultures and religions of these invaders have had an effect on the ideas and principles of Hinduism. Yet despite these many influences and the changes that came to pass, Hinduism has always absorbed the influences and remained the dominant religion of India.

THE GODS AND THE SCRIPTURES

At first sight Hinduism appears to be a polytheistic religion, meaning that its followers believe in many gods. Some people estimate the number of Hindu gods to be in the thousands. However, at the heart of Hinduism is really only one true "God"— Brahman. Brahman is also called the One, the Ultimate Reality, and the World Soul. The many gods traditionally found in Hinduism really form part of Brahman.

The Hindus have no single holy book, but an enormous body of sacred literature. Hinduism recognizes several sacred writings, all of which contribute to basic Hindu beliefs.

SHRUTI

The category of Hindu scriptures called *shruti* means "that which is heard." They consist of the Vedas, the Brahmanas, the Aranyakas, and the Upanishads. Each of the *shruti* texts provides an important part of the foundation of Hinduism.

Shruti and *Smriti*

There are two main categories of Hindu scripture—*shruti,* "that which is heard," and *smriti,* "tradition" or "that which is to be remembered." The Vedas and the Upanishads fall into the category of *shruti.* These sacred writings are considered to be inspired by God and to have been revealed to humankind by ancient sages called *rishis.*

The four Vedas are the oldest of the texts and are the primary scriptures of Hinduism. It is difficult to assign exact dates to these writings because many were compiled gradually over centuries, through oral tradition. They were written down only long after they had come into existence. Each of the four Vedas focuses on a particular subject or purpose. One contains hymns, chants, and praises to the gods. Another Veda serves as a guidebook for rituals and priestly behavior. A third offers information on magic and charms that can be used as blessings or curses, and the fourth gives musical notes to be chanted while performing the rituals. Together the four Vedas have had a deep and lasting influence on Hinduism.

The Brahmanas were texts composed after the Vedas. These texts give the details of the routines to be followed during the fire sacrifices. The Aranyakas, or the "forest books," were composed after the Brahamanas and emphasize the meaning behind the rituals of fire sacrifices.

The Upanishads, the latest of the *shruti* scriptures, were written around 700–500 B.C.E. One meaning for the word *Upanishad* is "sitting down near" a guru (spiritual master) who passes on his secret teachings. Almost all Upanishads are written in the form of dialogues between a student and a teacher. Indeed many of the Upanishadic teachings were to become permanent elements of Hinduism.

Most important of these are the concepts of karma (the idea that one's deeds will later have an effect in this life or in another life), samsara (reincarnation, or the cycles of a soul's birth and rebirth), and *moksha* (release from the cycles of samsara). In addition the Upanishads treated questions about the nature of both *atman* (the soul of the individual) and *brahman* (the Universal Soul), and their relationship to each other. These questions have played an important role in the development and practice of Hinduism.

Epics and Devotional Songs

Because of their divine origin *shruti* texts are considered to be more sacred than the other class of scriptures, *smriti*. Works that come after the Vedas and the Upanishads are all *smriti*. These include epics, the *puranas*, sutras, shastras, and devotional bhakti songs.

SMRITI

Smriti, the name of the second category of Hindu scriptures, means "that which is remembered." India boasts two great *smriti* epics. Both of them, the Mahabharata and the Ramayana, have had a significant influence on Hindu thought. These two epics have had many layers added to them over the centuries, but their core has essentially remained unchanged.

The Mahabharata consists of over 90,000 stanzas and is probably the longest epic poem in history. According to Hindu tradition the sage Vyasa dictated it to Ganesha, the elephant-headed god of good luck and the patron of learning. It tells the story of two families engaged in war. It includes the Bhagavad Gita, a sacred text spoken by the god Krishna to the hero Arjuna who is about to go into battle. It addresses the meaning and purpose of life and the nature of the indestructible soul. The text emphasizes the doctrine of the love (bhakti) between God and human-

A Hindu family offering *puja,* or daily worship, in front of a shrine laid with offerings, on the island of Bali in Indonesia. Although the majority of Hindus live in India, there are communities throughout Asia. Bali has more than 2.85 million Hindus, a third of the total Hindu population of Indonesia.

ity. The Bhagavad Gita is probably the single most influential text in contemporary Hinduism and was a major factor historically in shaping Hindu devotion.

The other great epic, the Ramayana ("The Adventures of Rama"), tells the tale of Rama, the seventh incarnation of the god Vishnu. The Ramayana depicts the ideals of faithfulness to marriage vows, brotherly affection, and loyalty. The earliest parts of the text date from around 350 B.C.E. Both the Mahabharata and the Ramayana have influenced the philosophy of Hinduism for over 2,000 years.

The *puranas*—literally "something very old"—are also *smriti* writings. Written in Sanskrit, these texts form a collection of verses that tell the stories of Hinduism's best-known gods and goddesses and the lives of ancient heroes. They include creation stories, portraits of the gods and famous sages, and accounts of time periods ruled by semigods called *manus*. They also speak of the end of the world and its rebirth, the history of humankind, and the legends of ancient dynasties. The *puranas* are referred to as the Vedas of the common people, because they present traditional religious and historical material through tales that most Hindus can understand.

Puja, Dharma, and *Samskara*

Some important rituals, beliefs, and traditions keep Hinduism vital and hold all of its traditions together. These are *puja,* or daily worship; dharma, religious duties pertaining to family and society; *samskara,* rites of passage; samsara, belief in the reincarnation or reappearance of the soul in succeeding generations; and *moksha,* or final release from material existence.

BHAKTI

Another popular form of scripture is the bhakti literature. These devotional songs were produced in both southern and northern regions of India, where teachers emphasized the love of those devoted to a personal god or goddess and the love returned by the god or goddess. The bhakti movement developed poet-sages who sang praises to Hindu gods and goddesses in the languages of the common people. By the sixth century C.E. these hymns were being sung in many temples. Many Hindus still write and sing bhakti hymns.

The Hindu scriptures and the stories they contain guide Hindus in their daily lives. They also help to preserve the religious dimensions of family and society. From these texts, and from their interpretations, Hindus have developed their system of worship and beliefs.

HINDU WORSHIP AND BELIEFS

Three major traditions comprise Hinduism, each based on a different idea of the divine, the universe, and the human condition. These each focus on the worship of a different personal representation of the Supreme—Shiva, Vishnu, or Shakti—and are referred to as Shaivism, Vaishnavism, and Shaktism, respectively. The different sects of Hinduism are loosely bound together by a single belief: They recognize that many different and individual paths may lead to the one ultimate goal of Hinduism, *moksha*, which is release from the attachment people have to this material world. Each lays out its own way of attaining *moksha's* reward—a blissful union with the universal spirit of Brahman.

Lighted oil lamps used during *puja*. Worshippers may perform a special kind of *puja* that involves all the senses. Lighted earthen lamps evoke the sense of sight; the sound of a bell evokes the sense of hearing; fragrant leaves and flowers evoke the sense of smell; ritual objects evoke the sense of touch; and finally, consumption of blessed food evokes the sense of taste.

PUJA

Each day Hindus worship the divine, through either a high god or a family deity. To do this they perform *puja* in a sacred section of a worship room of the home. The *puja* ritual keeps Hindus aware of their gods and mindful of their duties as individuals.

The most exalted setting for performing *puja* is the temple. The temple is the house of God and a link between human existence and the divine. It is also the center of social, artistic, intellectual, and religious affairs. Most essentially for a Hindu, the temple is a place that connects this world to the next.

THE CASTE SYSTEM

As early as the Vedic period Hindu society was roughly divided into four levels based on occupations. This basic part of Hindu life is known as the caste system. The Hindu caste system was supported by dharma, early religious laws of duty. Dharma insisted that particular castes had certain duties within the society. As a member of a caste an individual was responsible for upholding those duties. To neglect them was considered a sin that would upset the balance of life in the universe. Early Hindus believed, as do many modern Hindus, that if everyone were to perform his or her duty unquestioningly a balance could be maintained in the world and humans could exist in peace.

SAMSKARAS—THE FOUR STAGES OF LIFE

More recently the laws binding people to respect the caste system have been loosened. As a result modern dharma focuses more on duties to family than to society. Today the family unit is considered especially sacred, and the fulfillment of obligations to the family is a religious duty.

Within every family and throughout society individual life is divided into four stages—childhood, youth, middle age, and old age. Hindus practice *samskara*, traditional rites of passage, to mark these important transitions from the moment of conception to the time of death. All rites of passage, including those of death and afterlife, are performed at home by the head of the household, often aided by a Brahmin or family guru. According to tradition each family member is responsible for maintaining sacred order in the family, in society, and ultimately in the universe. The celebration of these rites of passage are part of that order. Religious observance of the basic rites (conception and

Moksha

In their pursuit of *moksha,* or release from material existence, Hindus share the ultimate goal of being spiritually united with the Ultimate Reality—Brahman. Thus Hindus consider the physical world to be unreal and only the world of mind and spirit to be real. To achieve *moksha* they seek inner peace and harmony in their lives. Hindus believe that all their actions and deeds will have some future effect—either in this life or in a future life of their souls. This idea is called the law of karma, and it governs all Hindu actions.

birth, introduction to the guru for initiation, marriage, and cremation after death) are believed to be part of the path that leads Hindus toward their goal of *moksha*—final release from material existence.

UNION WITH THE ULTIMATE REALITY

Because all human efforts and deeds are subject to the law of karma, Hindus try to erase their desires to achieve something in this utilitarian material world. This is because if they focus on achieving something in this material world, they will only prepare themselves for additional rebirths or new lives (samsara) in future generations on earth. Such efforts never lead to release from the material existence of this world. *Moksha* cannot be achieved by action aimed at gaining something in this world but only by an experience of oneself as united with God, the oneness of atman-Brahman, the union of one's self with the Ultimate Reality.

The way that Hindus resolve this problem is by the practice of *karmayoga,* namely by working for the sake of the Ultimate Reality. *Karmayoga,* taught in the Bhagavad Gita, means to work according to one's duty, but without attachment to the result. This path of selfless action leads ultimately to release from the cycle of birth and death.

CHAPTER 2

THE ROOTS OF HINDUISM

Hinduism was not always the complex religion it is today. Indologists, those who study the language, culture, and history of the Indian subcontinent, have theorized that it developed gradually as a merging of the beliefs and practices of two main groups—the people of the Indus Valley in India and the Aryans of Persia. The theory that Indo-Aryan migration was the key factor in the development of Hinduism, was put forward by European scholars in the 19th and early 20th centuries. That theory, however, is now the subject of much debate and should be considered only one possible interpretation of history.

Knowledge of the early stages of Hinduism comes from archaeological findings and from the earliest Hindu scriptures, the Vedas. Archaeological artifacts from the period around 1500 B.C.E. onward help us learn about the civilization of the Indus Valley both before and after the Aryan arrivals. They can tell us about both secular matters and spiritual life.

Cows along the banks of the sacred river Ganges. Roaming cows are a constant presence in Indian towns and cities. Cows and bulls are sacred not only because cows provide foods such as milk and cheese, but because cows were Krishna's companions. Bulls have been sacred since the times of the Indus Valley culture. Killing cows and bulls is a sin, and eating beef is sacrilegious.

From historical evidence we know that in this period early Hindu religious ideas were developed and clarified. Religion was a central part of life in the Indus Valley, and it helped to define the structure of society—the way individuals acted and interacted. Many of these ideas, both social and religious, still form a part of the basis of Hinduism.

INDUS VALLEY CIVILIZATION

About 5,000 years ago, in what is today Pakistan and northwestern India, a lively culture flourished on the banks of the Indus River. The Indus people lived in brick houses in well-planned villages. They were successful food cultivators who raised buffalo, goats, sheep, pigs, and dogs. They also exported cotton. Their comfortable civilization was built on a thriving agricultural and animal economy.

The Indus were governed by a strong, well-organized ruling class who had much concern for cleanliness, order, and stability. As we know from archaeological findings, personal hygiene and ritual cleanliness were of special importance to the Indus people. Each house in an Indus Valley village had a bathing room with drains. Also, there are numerous remains of bathing areas located in public places.

This drawing shows the elaborate headdress of an Indus Valley terra-cotta figurine.

The Great Bath and Ritual Purity

In one of the major Indus towns, Mohenjo Daro, was the Great Bath, a principal public structure. It contained a large water tank with entry steps leading downward at each end. Special rooms for private bathing surrounded the tank. Such rooms and a large water tank are still a common feature of modern Hindu temples.

RELIGIOUS LIFE OF THE INDUS VALLEY PEOPLE

Most information about the religious life of the Indus Valley people comes from the artifacts they have left behind. These include numerous small figures made of terra-cotta (baked earth) and seals, such as those found by archaeologists in two major towns, Mohenjo Daro and Harappa. These relics provide information about the beliefs of the Indus people as well as their craftsmanship. We know from the seals and figurines that the Indus people honored fertility, sexual power, and considered certain animals sacred.

It is not certain how the seals from Harappa and Mohenjo Daro were used. Many of the scenes depicted on the seals relate to the sacredness of sexual power and human creativity. Some scholars have indicated that whatever their use, the seals serve as evidence of the high quality of work produced by the two towns.

The terra-cotta figurines are so numerous that they seem to have been kept in nearly every home. Their craftsmanship is often rather crude when compared to the seals and some other small-scale sculptures found in public buildings of the Indus Valley. Because they are somewhat unrefined, family figurines may have been created by the common people for their own use rather than by expert craftsmen for use by the upper classes.

SYMBOL OF THE BULL

Other objects recovered from Harappa also support the idea that human sexual power and procreation were especially sacred to the people of the Indus Valley. Some, for example, depict various animals, such as bulls, or female figures engaged in sacred rituals. The bull is believed to be a symbol of virility and sexual power. It is a motif commonly depicted in Indus Valley art; out of more than 2,000 terra-cotta seals and seal impressions that have been found at the various archaeological sites, bulls predominate over other figures.

MOTHER GODDESSES

The most common types of figurines from the Indus Valley civilization represent what are often considered to be "mother goddesses." Almost all of these figures convey some idea of fertility and motherhood. They feature a female with wide hips, small breasts, tubular limbs, abundant jewelry, and an elaborate headdress. In some instances a small child appears on the hip or at the breast. In others a bulging abdomen suggests pregnancy.

A fertility figurine excavated in the Indus Valley. Such figurines are called "mother goddesses." A typical Indus Valley goddess has an elaborate headdress and tubular limbs.

THE FACES OF A FERTILITY GOD

One of the most striking sacred seals of the Harappan culture depicts a horned god who resembles the Hindu god Shiva. On the Harappan seals this god is seated in a very formal posture—perhaps a posture of meditation—with the soles of his feet pressed together. His arms extend away from the body, his thumbs rest on his knees, and the other fingers point downward. He wears elaborate ornaments and a peculiar headdress consisting of a pair of buffalo horns with a plantlike object between them. Around him are four wild animals—an elephant, a tiger, a rhinoceros, and a buffalo—and beneath his stool are two deer. The surrounding animals and the plantlike growth on his head indicate that he is a fertility god.

Although not all the animals depicted on the seals were considered sacred, the importance of the bull continues in later Hindu mythology, where it is associated with an important Hindu god, Shiva.

A PEACEFUL CIVILIZATION

From the artifacts of the Indus Valley we gain some insight into the peoples' lifestyle and sacred beliefs. These practices lasted for more than 1,000 years and would begin to form the basis of Hinduism. The Indus Valley also enjoyed a long, peaceful time, which makes the civilization's collapse somewhat puzzling and intriguing. As two possible causes, scholars look to climatic changes and to the gradual changing course of the Indus River and its tributaries. The Aryan migration from the steppes of eastern Europe through Persia could be another important cause of the collapse.

THE COMING OF THE ARYANS (INDO-EUROPEANS)

The Aryans were one of the many Indo-European tribes that migrated outward from the steppes of Central Asia. Some of the Aryan tribes journeyed across the mountains of Afghanistan into Pakistan and northwest India. There, more than 3,500 years ago, they confronted the Indus Valley civilization.

SEMINOMADIC WARRIORS

The Aryans were seminomadic warriors who came to Pakistan and northwest India in two-wheeled horse-drawn chariots. They brought a culture that sharply contrasted with that of the Indus people; the Aryans were skilled in bronze metalwork and had no interest in well-planned, fortified towns or agriculture or cattle raising. Although there is no evidence of Aryan architecture or of any art of quality and complexity, students of ancient civilization have excavated skillfully crafted metal weapons produced by this society.

The Aryans were patriarchal—they worshipped male gods. Goddess worship was unknown to them. Their major deities were gods who had links to the sun, for instance Indra, Varuna, and Agni. Aryan priests were poets who composed hymns in praise of their gods. Their hymns were intended to be sung during fire sacrifices made to appease the gods of the skies, the middle region, and the earth.

MERGING OF THE TWO CULTURES

Aryan literature was largely composed after the Aryans had settled in the Indus Valley. This literature clearly reflects the time when the Aryans confronted the Indus people. Some of their stories, for example, portray victories over a people called *dasas*—god-hating people addicted to strange religious rites. By the time the Aryans arrived in the Indus Valley, the Indus culture in the valley was showing increasing signs of disorder. However the Aryans did not enter a decayed cultural world. Many important religious elements, such as the reverence toward the Indus mother goddess, control over sexual power, and ritual cleanliness, persisted in Indus village cultures.

At first the Aryans ignored non-Aryan religious traditions. Later, however, they adopted some of the elements of Indus religions—those that their own religion could accommodate. Thus the Indus people and their beliefs gradually merged with the Aryan culture. The resulting culture was Aryan in structure, but it incorporated many local and non-Aryan beliefs and practices.

A row of lingam in a Hindu temple. The lingam is the most common manifestation of Shiva and represents his creative force. The abstract form of the male and female generative powers has been sacred from the time of the Indus Valley culture.

THE VEDAS AND THE VEDIC PERIOD

The Vedas were created by the Aryans who migrated toward northwest India from Persia. Like Hinduism itself these holy scriptures have acquired many cultural and chronological layers. Some Vedic thoughts are so old that they reflect an Iranian origin that predates the migration of the Aryans to India in 1500 B.C.E. Other ideas in the Vedas evolved while Aryans lived in the Indus Valley. The content of these older texts was absorbed by the Aryans when they came to dominate the different cultures of the Indus Valley. There are four Vedas, the oldest and primary scriptures of Hinduism. The Vedas provide much historical, sociological, religious, and linguistic information about the people who composed them. They also provide a foundation for many Hindu religious concepts.

AN ORAL TRADITION

For centuries the Vedas were passed by teachers to students through an oral tradition. Even when an alphabet was introduced

Archaeological remains of Mohenjo Daro, one of the major towns in the Indus Valley civilization. A major source of information about religious life in the Indus Valley comes from objects that have been found there.

there was strong opposition to committing the Vedas to writing. The Brahmins (priests) believed that the power of the holy Vedic hymns lay in the tradition of hearing the text, thus the name for such hymns: *shruti*, or "that which is heard." Memorizing the Vedas from written words, according to the Brahmins, brought one great religious strength. Eventually, however, for the sake of preservation, these holy hymns

Veda

The word *veda* means "knowledge." The knowledge that the Vedas contain was considered to be of divine origin, revealed by the creator-god Brahman. Sages, or *rishis*, were given the responsibility of transmitting the divine gift to humankind.

THE FOUR VEDAS

Rig Veda

The Rig Veda is by far the oldest collection of hymns. Although a precise date for its origin is impossible to pinpoint, scholars estimate that elements of the text span a time range from 5000 B.C.E.to 900 B.C.E. The Rig Veda contains hymns and praises to the gods.

Yajur Veda

The second Veda, composed around 700 B.C.E., is called the Yajur Veda. It contains a variation of the Rig Veda text. In addition it provides details for performing sacrifices, building altars, and reciting ritual phrases. In essence, it is the Brahmins' handbook.

Sama Veda and Atharva Veda

The two remaining Vedas—Sama Veda and Atharva Veda—contain significant portions of the Rig Veda, and both offer supplementary guidelines for priestly behavior. However some differences do exist between these two Vedas. Parts of the Sama Veda, for example, center on sacrifices to Soma, a god of enthusiasm and intoxication whose worship developed from an undiscovered stimulant akin to the intoxication brought on by certain wild mushrooms. The hymns of the Atharva Veda are more concerned with magic spells, charms, and incantations. These fall into one of two categories: those of a healing, medicinal nature, such as love potions, cure-alls, and blessings; and those of a negative character, calling down misfortune or sickness upon enemies.

VARUNA

The sky god Varuna was one of the most important gods of the early Vedic period. He was the overseer of moral action, and his guidance was the standard for cosmic, moral, and religious order. This order is called *rita*. Varuna created the world and ruled it by the standard of *rita*. *Rita* also provided a structure for other celestial *devas*.

The following is a Vedic hymn offered to Varuna:

Forgive, O gracious Lord, forgive!
Whatever sin we mortals have committed
against the people of the gods; if, foolish,
we have thwarted your decrees, O god, do
not destroy us in your anger!

—Basham 240

Vishnu

Vishnu was a minor celestial god during the early Vedic period. Later Vishnu would become one of the three major gods of Hinduism. His main distinction in the Vedas was the three strides by which he crossed the earth, the atmosphere, and then reached "the highest place," his special heaven. This ability was a significant factor in his later rise to prominence.

were written in an old form of Sanskrit that we now call Vedic. There are four collections of Vedas, the Rig Veda, the Yajur Veda, the Sama Veda, and the Atharva Vedathe. The collections include hymns, rules for performing rituals, guidelines on priestly behavior, and magic spells and incantations.

DEVAS—A COMMUNITY OF DIVINE POWERS

Early Vedic religion centered on divine power. The gods, called *devas,* comprised a pantheon (community) of divine powers. The number of the gods was not important—rather the functions of the gods or the way they were associated with natural events or phenomena were important. *Devas* were classified as celestial, atmospheric, or terrestrial, depending on the primary location of their activity: sky, atmospheric region, or earth.

CELESTIAL GODS

The Vedic people believed in many celestial gods: Varuna, the guardian of cosmic law; Mitra, Varuna's chief assistant and a friend and benefactor of humankind; Surya, who represented the physical aspect of the sun; and Savitri, who represented the sun's ability to stimulate life.

To invite the celestial gods down to earth, into their special places of prayer and worship, the early Hindus performed rituals. The god was honored with an offering of food and hymns of praise. A typical sacrificial hymn contained an invocation, or calling, to the god, offered in a tone of friendliness, reverence, or fear—depending on the god and one's relation to the god.

ATMOSPHERIC GODS

Hindus of the early Vedic period also believed in another class of devas. These were the atmospheric gods who included Indra, the god of lightning and thunder; Vayu, the god of wind; the Maruts, a troop of storm gods; and Rudra, the father of the Maruts.

Indra, a model warrior, was a figure of great popularity and prestige. In fact he was the second most important god of the early Vedic era. The key to his character was a myth describing his conquest of the demon Vritra, a serpentine monster who blocked the flow of life-giving waters to the Aryans. It is said that Indra not only slew this mythic enemy; he also fought the real enemies of the Aryans, the *dasas,* or slaves, of the Indus Valley. Indra is called the Fortress Splitter and is praised for his destruction of the fortified citadels of Aryan opponents. With his belly full of exhilarating drink and his thunderbolt ready, Indra represented what an Aryan warrior aspired to be.

Rudra, the father of the Maruts, or storm gods, was feared because of his malevolent and destructive nature. He was also praised at times for his ability to protect his people from misfortune by sending storms upon their enemies. Rudra was a minor *deva,* far overshadowed by Varuna and Indra during this early Vedic period. In later Hinduism, however, his characteristics merged with the qualities of a non-Aryan, Indus Valley deity— an early form of the god Shiva. He then became one of the three major Hindu gods.

In the great Hindu epic the Mahabharata, the god Vishnu rose to prominence alongside the gods Brahma and Shiva. Vishnu is pictured here with four arms. In his lower hand he carries a club signifying power and protection, in his raised right had he holds a chakra or wheel representing the cycle of life and death and in his raised left hand he holds a conch shell whose spiral shape represents infinite space.

CHAPTER 3

THE LATE VEDIC PERIOD AND THE UPANISHADIC PERIOD

Around the 15th century B.C.E. Aryan tribes migrated slowly across the plains of northern India to the Ganges Valley. By about the end of the ninth century B.C.E. Aryans as well as non-Aryans occupied the whole of the Ganges Valley. They were organized into distinct principalities, or states. Some were ruled by hereditary rulers called rajas. Others, who were still in community groups of largely non-Aryan clans, were governed by chieftains. The principalities were populated by people of various ethnic compositions. There were light-skinned Aryans, dark-skinned Indus Valley people, and local tribal people of the Ganges Valley who had distinct skin coloration.

In the areas they occupied, the Aryans formed the upper level of a still-fluid social order. Below them were the non-Aryans. Although this separation among the classes was not hard and fast, the Brahmins distinguished four classes of people: Brahmins, the priests; the ruling Rajanyas or Kshatriyas who, for the most part, were warriors; the Vaishyas, or common people such as

Female friends and family members celebrate their arrival as pilgrims to bathe in the waters of the sacred river Ganges.

artisans and farmers; and the Shudras, servants who are thought to have been non-Aryan natives. The belief in separate classes, the caste system, was supported and given religious sanction by a hymn in the Vedic scripture. There also developed a fifth group of people who carried out the most menial jobs in society such as clearing away dead bodies. They formed the 'untouchable' castes which are now called Dalit (downtrodden) and officially known as Scheduled Castes.

In the late Vedic period the worldview gradually changed. Major gods of the early Vedic period lost their importance. In later Vedic writings interest shifted away from celestial and atmospheric gods toward *devas* who were located on the land. Also, more attention was directed toward sacrificial rituals.

Offerings over a fire during *puja*. Agni is the god of fire from the Vedic period and became the sacrificial fire itself. Fire remains one of the central elements of Hindu ritual.

It was during this period that the Brahmins, or priests, gained importance and power in early Hindu society. Eventually people came to question the Brahmins' role. The period following the Vedic period, the era of the Upanishads, showed the results of this questioning.

Through the Upanishadic era the religious history of the Hindus was never static. There had been a dynamic process of growth and innovation throughout the early period. From the hymns of the Vedas to the compilations of the Brahmanas and the Aranyakas (the "forest books"), there was a constant growth that followed the changing times of the society. The Upanishadic period likewise was vibrant with new ideas, speculation, and knowledge. The rejection of beliefs with which people could not identify and the quest for new answers filled the teachings of the Upanishads and inspired new thought.

TERRESTRIAL GODS AND THE IMPORTANCE OF SACRIFICE

Sacrifice became an important part of Hindu life in the late Vedic period approximately 3,000 years ago. As a result only gods directly associated with sacrifices—such as Agni, the god of fire; Soma, the god of sacrificial libation or the pouring of drinks; and Brahaspati, the divine priest and lord of prayer—retained the interest of the later Vedic priests. In this later era Varuna, Indra, and others only received minor sacrifices.

FIRE SACRIFICE RITUALS

During this era the religious life of the Hindus became increasingly dominated by the rituals and traditions performed around a fire pit. These so-called fire sacrifice rituals gradually became extremely sophisticated and complex. Fire was now believed to be the creative source of all the powers of the gods and of nature. Fire rituals were of two kinds: *griha,* domestic rituals performed by the householder or priests, and *shrauta,* specialized rites performed by priests for patrons who paid for the sacrifice.

Gradually the distinction between the *shrauta* and *griha* rituals became blurred, because both types of rites were subject to priestly influence and control. Even though *griha* rituals could be performed at home, they were still taught and controlled by priests. Interestingly, most domestic rituals have been handed down from Vedic times to the present with little change or addition. Today, however, priests do not control the *griha* rituals.

Shrauta

In *shrauta* rituals Vedic hymns were recited by the Brahmin. The *shrauta* sacrifices were complicated, and over time they became more and more elaborate and complex. Sacrificial duties then had to be divided among several priests. Performing the sacrifice, once meant to be a celebration of the *devas,* gradually came to be viewed as bringing power in its own right. Thus priests came to hold a lot of power in Hindu society.

Griha

While rites performed by priests became more complicated, *griha,* or domestic rites, remained simple. They celebrated the new and full moons, the seasons of the year, and the first fruit of the harvest, or they marked special family occasions such as the building of a new house, the birth of a son, and the passage through important stages of life. *Griha* rites could be performed on a household fire maintained by a pious parent, following the rituals spelled out over the years by the priests.

AGNI—THE FIRE GOD

During fire sacrifices people offered their possessions to the gods. The most important sacrificial offerings were placed in a fire. People believed that the god Agni conveyed their offerings to the other gods through the fire. Agni was thought to be both the god of fire and the sacrificial fire itself. As the god of fire he was the medium through which humans could relate directly to the other gods.

Agni quickly became an all-important deity. In the celestial region Agni was the sun. In the atmospheric region he was lightning. Finally, by lightning he was brought to the earth, and rekindled as fire from the trees in which he was hidden. When *shrauta* rituals were performed three kinds of fire were kept so that they might symbolically represent Agni of the sky, of the atmosphere, and of the earth.

SOUND AND SACRED ACTIONS

In the late Vedic period other sacrificial elements also grew in importance. In particular the element of sound and the sacred actions accompanying repetitive sound became essential to the sacrifice.

During the offering of sacrifices ritual statements referred to as mantras, or verse prayers, were recited. Mantras were thought to capture the power of Brahman, the Upanishadic Ultimate Reality. Because of their deep wisdom, and often because of their magical power, the mantras or the sacred speech soon became more important to know than the natural world. Eventually sacred speech was deified in the form of the goddess Vac (meaning "speech").

LINK TO THE DIVINE WORLD

In sacrifices Agni represented all the other gods. As the messenger to them Agni linked humankind to the divine world. Because he could assume various forms of fire, Agni was believed to be an example of the divine world throughout nature.

*You, O Agni, are Indra, the bull of all
    that exists;
You are the wide striding Vishnu,
    worthy of reverence;
O Lord of the Holy Word (Brahaspati),
    you are the chief priest.
. . . You, O Agni, are King Varuna,
    whose laws are firm;
You are Mitra, the wonder-worker to
    be revered . . .
You, O Agni, are Rudra, the Asura of
    lofty heaven;
As the troops of Maruts, you control
    sustenance.*

—Rig Veda II.1, 3, 4, 6 Hopkins 18

SACRIFICES OF THE GODS

The gods themselves are said to have performed sacrifices to obtain their places in the Vedic heaven. Although the early Vedas are not known for stories of creation, there is such a story at the end of the oldest and most important one, the Rig Veda. The story is known as the "Hymn of the Primeval Man."

The story told of a god known as Prajapati, the lord of beings, who was also known as Purusha. It was believed that he existed before the foundation of the universe. Prajapati was a primeval human being who was sacrificed by the gods, who were his children. From the body of this divine victim the universe was created.

HYMN OF THE PRIMEVAL MAN

The "Hymn of the Primeval Man," from the Rig Veda, describes the first cosmic sacrifice, which brought forth the universe. According to the poem the sacrifice of Purusha, the cosmic victim, is the reference point for all things. His sacrifice is the key to creation. Early Hindus believed that all other sacrifices were imitations of this great sacrifice. Furthermore they believed that to know Purusha's sacrifice was to know the universe:

When the gods made a sacrifice with the Man (Purusha) as their victim, Spring was the melted butter, Summer the fuel, and Autumn the oblation. From that all-embracing sacrifice the clotted butter was collected. From it he made the animal of air and wood and village. From that all-embracing sacrifice were born the hymns and chants, from that the meters were born, from that the sacrificial spells were born. Thence were born horses, and all beings with two rows of teeth. Thence were born cattle, and thence goats and sheep. When they divided the Man, into how many parts did they divide him? What was his mouth, what were his arms, what were his thighs and his feet called? The Brahmin was his mouth, of his arms was made the Kshatriya, his thighs became the Vaishya, of his feet the Shudra was born. The moon arose from his mind. From his eye was born the sun. From his mouth Indra and Agni. From his breath the wind was born. From his navel came the air. From his head there came the sky, from his feet the earth, the four quarters from his ear. Thus they fashioned the world. With Sacrifice the gods sacrificed to sacrifice. These were the first of the sacred laws. The mighty beings reached the sky, where are the eternal spirits, the gods.

—Basham 242–243

In this poem, parallels are made between Purusha's sacrificed body and all the levels of creation. All creation is given a religious association in which Purusha, the cosmic victim, is centrally important. The cosmos, the world of nature, human society, and sacrifice are seen as similar and parallel, all created at the same time for all ages by Purusha's sacrifice.

BRAHMINS AND POWER

Throughout much of the Vedic period the Brahmins (priests) held a central place of power in society. This was in part because the Brahmins controlled and oversaw the sacrifices in which the gods came down to earth to partake in offerings by their devotees. As mentioned, these included *shrauta* and *griha* rituals. The Brahmins also held additional power because they controlled knowledge of the Vedas.

A Hindu offering prayers at a temple in southern India. Close to her feet is a small ritual fire.

BRAHMINS AND THE VEDAS

The Vedas were passed from teacher to student in the oral tradition. They had to be studied and memorized by priests and then told to members of other castes. Because of this members of the priestly caste could literally hold the knowledge within their caste. Brahmins not only knew the sacrificial hymns and prayers by heart, but they were considered to be the only specialists qualified to perform the holy fire sacrifices for the people. Thus the Brahmins controlled common access to the gods and ultimately to the entire cosmos.

By the end of the Vedic period the Brahmins had made a supplementary addition to each of the four Vedas. These four compilations were called Brahmanas. They contained guidance for priests in the use of hymns and prayers. The Brahmanas gave practical directions, in great detail, for carrying out all types of sacrifice.

To explain the deeper meaning of these complex rites still more explanations had to be compiled. These further explanations were known as Aranyakas, or forest books, because the teaching of them took place in forest retreats. Although the Brahmanas insisted on proper ritual actions, the Aranyakas seemed to claim that the understanding of the meaning behind the ritual actions was more important. They claimed that perfect ritual did not depend on elaborate fire sacrifices but could be performed

THE ORIGIN OF CREATION

The following hymn contains an alternative explanation for the creation of the universe. It clearly questions the early Vedic vision of creation:

Then there were neither death nor immortality,
Nor was there then the torch of night and day.
That One breathed windlessly and self-sustaining;
There was that One then, and there was no other.
At first there was only darkness wrapped in darkness;
All this was only unillumined water.
That one which came to be, enclosed in nothing,
Arose at last, born of the power of heat (tapas).
In the beginning desire (Kama, creative or
sacrificial impulse) descended on it —
that was the primal seed, born of the mind . . .
But, after all, who knows, and who can say
Whence it all came, and how creation happened?
The gods themselves are later than creation,
So who knows truly whence it has arisen?
Whence all creation had its origin?
He, whether he fashioned it or whether he did not,
He, who surveys it all from highest heaven,
He knows, or perchance he knows not.

—Rig Veda X.129.6, 7

within one's own mind. The compilation of the Brahmanas and Aranyakas clearly shows how fascinated and absorbed the Vedic priests were with their rituals and the process of elaborating on them and interpreting them.

PROPER PERFORMANCE OF RITUALS

The use of the Brahmanas' rituals was limited to those who were considered to be ritually pure and fit. A knowledge of the proper ritual actions brought people offering sacrifices into the company of those having direct access to the gods. If the rituals were properly performed by the priests throughout their lives, it was believed that after death both the priests and those who asked them to offer the sacrifices would be rewarded with an existence freed from their mortal bodies. In short, they would be elevated to the world of the gods.

Over time many people became disenchanted with the complex rituals that the Brahmins prescribed. Also, the idea that the universe was formed and maintained through Purusha's sacrifice lost religious support. Different ideas about the world's creation and life's meaning gained attention.

One widely believed theory stated that the world could be explained in terms of a neutral, or impersonal, principle. This principle was known simply as "that One."

ASCETICS

As a result of spiritual and social questioning, a way of life quite in contrast to all the complex rituals of the Brahmins became increasingly common at this time. This was the lifestyle of people known as ascetics. Ascetics are dedicated to great austerity and self-discipline in their lives. In late Vedic times they tended to live as hermits in the forest and chose not to participate in the Hindu social structure with its many castes.

Ascetics emerged from all sections of society and rivaled the Brahmins in commanding the highest respect of the people. The passion that fueled the austere devotion of the ascetic in the forest was itself revered as sacrificial; this passionate dedication to the austere life was compared to a fire on the altar. The repetition of Vedic chants that characterized the lives of the Vedic priests was thought to be equivalent to the austere devotion of these ascetics. The heat of such ascetic devotion and prayer was called *tapas,* or the heat of knowledge. The simple and sincere acts of the ascetics were thought to bring a higher understanding of the Ultimate Reality. Indeed, it allowed the ascetics to have a higher understanding of all reality.

Because ascetics led lives of austerity and purity, it was believed that they could generate "the heat of deep knowledge" by their acts of meditation and by their ascetic practices. People began

QUIET THINKING

The ascetics, or forest hermits, were adept in various forms of meditation, or quiet thinking. Some were called *munis* (silent ones) and others *rishis* (having the power of knowledge). The *munis* were described as those who ". . . wear the wind as a girdle, and who are drunk with their own silence. They know the thoughts of all the people, for they have drunk the magic cup of Rudra/Shiva, which is poison to ordinary mortals."

A Hindu ascetic offering *puja* at a small shrine in a simple shelter.

to believe more and more that without priests they themselves could experience the power of meditation and ascetic practice to bring on deep religious knowledge. Meditation and asceticism were seen as keys to religious fervor and they were available to forest hermits as well as to those who wanted to imitate their activities.

A LIFE NOT RULED BY DEATH

The religious example of the ascetics presented an alternative religious form of life for many people. The Vedic tradition of the Brahmins seemed centered on the priests and the exact performance of their rituals. Having become to some degree disenchanted with the elaborate sacrifices of the Brahmins, many people wanted to know if there was some higher goal to life than offering exactly performed sacrifices. People began to search for a state of immortality, a life not ruled by death and not eroded by time. They also wondered how such a state could be obtained— how they might transcend or overcome the defeating condition of a life where there seemed to be no hope of something greater. Hindus of the Upanishadic period tried to answer some of these new religious questions.

THE UPANISHADIC PERIOD

The Upanishadic period (800–450 B.C.E.) was one of the greatest eras of creative thinking in the history of Hinduism. During this period people took a more questioning attitude toward human existence. Upanishadic ascetics were philosophers, teachers, and seers. They lived in forest hermitages. They spent their days studying, contemplating, and discussing the puzzling questions of the universe. Young minds were attracted to these hermitages, hoping to engage in debates there and thus find enlightenment.

SITTING DOWN NEAR THE GURU

The Upanishads were composed by these forest hermits around 700–500 B.C.E., as the last section of the Vedas. They are also known as *shruti,* or "listened-to" texts, and almost all of their teachings are in the form of dialogues. The meaning of the word *Upanishad* is "sitting down near" a guru (spiritual master) who passes on his secret teachings. More than 100 compilations of these dialogues are written down, though only 13 of them are accepted as *smriti*, or sacred scriptures. Generally the Upanishads discuss the relationship between the individual and the universe, the nature of the universal soul, the meaning of life, and the character of life after death.

The Upanishadic period introduced to Hinduism a new and influential kind of thinking and questioning. In principle these texts differed from the Vedas in that they did not exclude people outside the Brahmin caste. However the content of the Upanishads is subtle and profound. Since understanding the Upanishadic concepts has been considered a difficult task, only a few in fact come to a deep knowledge of their teachings.

Despite the complexity of the Upanishads men and women of all classes participated in Upanishadic learning. It was not one's class or caste but one's character that was important. Honesty, for example, was much more highly valued in a potential student at a hermitage than was a person's family tree.

STAYING WITH THE TRUTH

One passage from the Chandogya Upanishad poignantly expresses how much the inner person was appreciated within the religious community that studied the Upanishads:

Satyakama was the son of a woman named Jabala. One day her son asked, "Mother, I want to be a student. What is my family name?" His mother replied, "My dear, I don't know your family. I had you when I was very young traveling as a servant. My name is Jabala, and yours is Satyakama, so you are Satyakama Jabala." The next day the boy went to a teacher named Gautama Haridrumata, and said: "I want to be your student, sir. Can I?" The teacher asked what his family name was. Satyakama replied, "I don't know my family, sir. I asked my mother and she said that she had me in her youth, when she traveled about a lot as a servant. . . She said she was Jabala and I was Satyakama and that I was to give my name as Satyakama Jabala." The teacher replied, "Nobody but a true brahman would be so honest!" He said, "Go and fetch me fuel, my friend, and I will initiate you, for you have not swerved from the truth."

—Chandogya Upanishad IV.4

CREATIVE POWERS AND A DIVINE LINK

Two of the oldest (ca. 700–500 B.C.E.) and most significant of the Upanishadic scriptures are the Brihadaranyaka Upanishad and the Chandogya Upanishad. In the Chandogya Upanishad, a question is posed so that its answer can show the relationship between the sacrificial fire on the altar, the fire in the sun, and *tapas.* The question is about the creative powers in the universe. It is formulated in this way: What is the nature of the One that is the cause of the whole of existence? The answer discusses the creative powers of *tapas,* of sacrifice, and of the ultimate truth, Brahman.

Students of the Upanishads believed that it was not the ritual acts of sacrifices themselves, but rather the spirit behind the sacrifices that was important. They believed that through meditation or reflection they could attain the knowledge of how they were related to the gods and how this divine link originated. They also wanted to know what were their real selves and what was the relationship of their real selves to the Universal Reality, that is, Brahman.

TRANSCENDING WORLDLY CARES

Such spiritual reflection and searching was believed to cause *tapas* within the dedicated student. By setting aside all other concerns, the student really was "sacrificing" them. In this respect these individuals set aside or "sacrificed" worldly concerns and thereby performed sacrifices on the altar of their hearts. Such self-sacrifices paralleled the fire sacrifices of the Vedic priests.

Upanishadic ascetics sacrificed their selves, disciplined their bodily concerns, and desired enlightenment. They believed that this showed a power to transcend worldly cares and contemplate the important questions of reality. Such practices led to a belief that an individual had, beyond a surface self, an essential or real self. The question then was to ask what this essential self was and how one could grasp it. This question, which is still important in modern Hinduism, was answered in part by a new idea of the Ultimate.

THE BRAHMAN AND THE ATMAN

A major focus of the Upanishadic thinkers was the idea that an individual's soul, called atman, was a separated part of Brahman, or the universal soul. Since the Upanishadic era an important theme of Hinduism has been this belief in the oneness of the individual soul and the Universal Soul. The separated atman, after achieving *moksha,* or salvation, will be united again with Brahman. Eventually the word *Brahman* was used to refer to the universal essence containing all kinds of power.

The idea of atman-Brahman is repeated in the famous phrase from the Chandogya Upanishad, *"tat tvam asi,"* literally, "that thou art." This phrase means that there is no difference between the individual and the universal.

The identity of the soul of the individual and the soul of the universe is the central theme throughout the Upanishadic texts. *Tat tvam asi,* "you (the individual soul) are that (the universal essence)" is the principal teaching of the period.

SAMSARA, KARMA, AND *MOKSHA*

Of the many Upanishadic teachings that were to become permanent elements of Hinduism, those of samsara and karma are among the most prominent.

PASSING OF A SOUL FROM BODY TO BODY

Samsara is a belief in the transmigration, or continual passing, of a soul from one body to another. It can be described as follows. The soul of a person who dies does not pass into heaven, or hell, or elsewhere. It is reborn into another body, which may be of a higher or lower order than one's

Brahman—the Supreme Essence

In the Upanishads all the many gods of the Vedic tradition are reduced to one, Brahman. Brahman was believed to be the supreme essence of the universe. This essence is seen in the universe, in the various creations of the physical world, and in the soul of individuals.

Young Brahman boys performing *puja* on a stone statue of Vishnu resting on a serpent at Buddhalakinath in the Kathmandu Valley, Nepal.

THE ESSENCE OF SELF

A story from the Brihadaranyaka Upanishad illustrates that there is no difference between the individual and the universal.

"Put this salt in water, and come to me in the morning." The student did as he was told. In the morning the teacher said, "Fetch the salt." The student looked for it, but could not find it, because it had dissolved. "Taste the water from the top, said the teacher. "How does it taste?" "Of salt," the student replied. "Taste from the middle. How does it taste?" "Of salt," the student replied. "Taste from the bottom. How does it taste?" "Of salt," the student answered. Then the teacher said, "You don't perceive that one Reality exists in your own body, my dear, but it is truly there. Everything which has its being is that subtle essence. That is Reality! That is the Soul! And you are that, Svetaketu!"

previous existence. Rebirth follows rebirth in an endless chain. Thus a person of low status may be reborn as a priest, or a king, or an animal, or even a worm. The question then arises: What causes the soul to enter a higher or lower state of existence?

THE LAW OF DEEDS

A person's higher or lower state of existence is determined by the law of karma (the law of deeds or works.) This is a law determining that an individual's thoughts, words, and deeds have ethical consequences that establish the quality of the person's future existences. For Hindus the law of karma is a necessary law of nature. It decides the quality of a Hindu's further life. A person who has done good deeds is reborn into a good existence in the next birth, and if he or she has done bad deeds the person achieves a less fortunate birth.

Karma does not only apply to one's future life; it also applies to what happens in one's present life. According to the law of karma the good that a person does in this life eventually comes back to him or her in the form of good fortune, either in one's present life or in one's future existence. Likewise a person pays a "karmic price" for the evil deeds he or she might have performed. The evil deed will come back to "haunt" the person in this present life or in a future existence.

RELEASE TO UNION WITH THE BRAHMAN

The highest of the Upanishadic teachings completes the ideas of samsara and karma. This is the concept of *moksha,* or release: by leading a good spiritual life—that is, by union with Brahman, or the Ultimate Reality—an individual will eventually leave the temporary existences and the cycle of samsara. With the idea of *moksha* the desire for eternal oneness with Brahman became more important than improving one's position in this life or gaining physical enjoyment by good deeds or karma.

In the Upanishadic era Hindus gradually placed an increasingly higher value on the goal of union with the Universal Soul and release from the realm of samsara. *Moksha* came to be considered the highest and perhaps the sole purpose of life. Over the years various Hindu sects strove toward this same goal, but they did so through different methods.

YOGA AND VEDANTA

Along with the new ideas of sacrifice, God, and the cycle of samsara, the Upanishadic period also saw many new schools of religious philosophy. One of these was yoga. Yoga is a form of physical and mental discipline. Although its practice was much older than the Upanishads, the common methods of yoga were further developed and explained in this era. Upanishadic seers followed yogic techniques that emphasized the difference between the body and the self.

Vedanta was another powerful school of religious philosophy that emerged at this time. It fostered the idea that there was an underlying unity to all reality. It introduced the concept of *maya*, an impersonal force that makes people forget that all individuals are part of the universal essence. *Maya* is believed to be the cause of all ignorance and suffering and must be overcome.

NEW METHODS OF TEACHING

The instruction of the Upanishads promised a religious teaching that would be

A sadhu, a Hindu holy man who has renounced the material world, can usually be recognized by matted, tangled hair and the most simple possession such as a loose cloak and a wooden staff. He has let go of his social status in order to find the highest truth (Brahman) through mental and physical discipline. His goal is to be spiritually united with Brahman in order to achieve salvation, *moksha*.

Jivanmukta

Those who practiced yoga believed that it could lead them to a state in which atman, the individual soul, became one with Brahman, the universal soul. This was possible because the self in its deepest reality was believed already to be like Brahman—pure, limitless, and unchanging. People who practiced yoga and had this special experience of union with Brahman were called *jivanmukta* (those who are liberated while still alive).

Praying before a shrine to Nandi, the sacred white bull who is ridden by Shiva. *Nandi* means "he who grants joy" and this bull represents the inner strength that is gained by controlling physical needs and letting go of violence and anger.

centered on ordinary people and not on the detailed sacrificial rites of the Brahmins. However, many common people had difficulty understanding the texts. The Upanishadic teachings were simply too philosophical and puzzling. During the same time as the Upanishadic period, some non-Brahmin thinkers, such as Buddhists, came to reject the old sacrificial tradition of the Brahmins. These teachers began to convey their religious lessons in new ways—through the telling of stories and parables.

STORIES OF TRAVELING TEACHERS

Coming out of the confines of the forest schools that had been the classrooms of the Upanishads, the new teachers traveled from one town to the next. While traveling they told stories and spread their beliefs and ideas. The people listened eagerly and were entranced by the simple parables. They found the teachings uplifting. They also discovered that the stories brought them understanding of their lives and of the world.

Soon the stories and parables, which often illustrated moral or religious lessons, became very popular. Seeing that this approach to religious teaching was successful, even the Brahmins began to adopt storytelling as part of their preaching method. Consequently new forms of Brahmanic literature came into existence around the third century B.C.E. At that time the Brahmins wrote new literature as well as additions to older works. Some examples of how the Brahmins adapted the new teaching methods can be seen in the additions they made to the great epic poems, the Ramayana and the Mahabharata, and also to the sacred writings known as the *puranas.*

STORIES OF THE GODS

Whereas the epics seem to have reached their final form by 500 C.E., the *puranas* continued to develop until late in the 12th century C.E. The *puranas,* or "old stories," incorporate legends, myths, and customary observances. Later portions of the *puranas* focused on stories of the gods Brahma, Vishnu, and Shiva. Hindus worshipped each of these three gods separately, but the three were also considered to be one god with three functions: creation (Brahma), preservation (Vishnu), and destruction (Shiva).

The myths and legends of the *puranas* brought meaning to people's lives. Because the legends were often intertwined with significant historical facts, the *puranas* were often associated with *itihasa* (history). Like the epics, *puranic* texts are considered important because they have been, and still are, the media of mass education in the Hindu world. For centuries religious, social, and cultural norms and inspirations have been imparted through this type of literature.

HEROES AND LEGENDS

The Ramayana and Mahabharata are the repositories in story form of the essential wisdom of all that went before. Originally the Ramayana and the Mahabharata were long stories about the exploits and struggles of warriors and kings told by generations of traveling bards. All sorts of material was included in these basic stories so that each of the great epics, especially the Mahabharata, developed into an encyclopedia of heroes and legends—some legends giving historical portraits, some creating mythological images. It is in the epics that one encounters the ever-developing characters of the great gods Shiva and Vishnu, in the form of his avatars Rama and Krishna, their wives, their families, and numerous other minor gods.

"GREAT OLD STORIES AND GLORIFICATIONS"

While many works may bear the name *purana,* only 18 are traditionally acknowledged as *shruti,* or sacred. These are called the *mahapuranas,* "great old stories." It is also true that any religious text could be called a minor *purana.* Many minor *puranas* that were written after the older *shruti* were referred to as *mahatmyas,* or "glorifications." These mostly glorified gods and places of pilgrimage. Among these are modern *mahatmyas,* some composed as recently as the 19th century.

CHAPTER 4

THE GODS AND RELIGIOUS DEVOTION

During the period 500 B.C.E. to 400 C.E. the *puranas* were inspired by many Hindu traditions. Within each tradition individuals considered one god to be their personal god and the highest god. What developed with this more personal religious perspective was a popular devotional movement known as bhakti, which means "attachment," or a fervent devotion to a god.

The seeds of this new approach to religion had been sown in the earlier traditions of both the epics and the *puranas*. We can see how the seeds developed if we study some of the stories of the gods and the people's new appreciation of certain gods. In the earlier periods these gods had small roles within the Hindu pantheon. They took on new dimensions and gained in importance as the years moved on.

THE AMBIGUOUS GOD SHIVA

Shiva was not a prominent god in the earlier writings of the Brahmins. In the Vedas the forerunner of the god Shiva was the terrible atmospheric *deva* Rudra, an Aryan god of storms, lightning, and medicinal herbs. Because Rudra controlled atmospheric forces

A illustration from the epic poem called the Ramayana ("The Adventures of Rama") showing the wedding procession of Rama and Sita. Rama is the seventh avatar or incarnation of the god Vishnu.

the Indus Valley people believed that he could direct human destiny. In return for the prayers of his worshippers Rudra gave them healing remedies and protected them against the destruction brought by powerful storms.

THE TRADITION OF SHIVA WORSHIP

By the period of the Upanishads Rudra's characteristics merged with those of another Indus Valley terrestrial god of cattle to form Shiva, one of three major gods. He was the Indus yogic god having control over sexuality. He was the Vedic god of terrible rains and storms and the healing god of herbs. In addition he was the deity of animals, the father of storm gods, and the god of yogic power. He became known for his contradictory powers, particularly sexual power and the power of yogic self-control. Religious

A painting showing the male and female aspects of Shiva. Many myths provide absorbing portraits of Shiva's multisided nature. These myths occur often in the epics and the *puranas*. Each time the stories are told a bit differently, depending on the storyteller and the time they were written down.

awe of the complex figure of Shiva and his wife, Parvati, merged into the tradition of Shiva worship—referred to as Shaivism—during the early decades (third century B.C.E.) of the *puranic* time period.

In the Mahabharata Shiva is worshipped not only as creator of the universe but also as the primeval father. The great epic tells of Shiva living in the Himalayas with his wife, Parvati (a beneficent and mild form of the great goddess Mahadevi Shakti), and their two sons, Ganesha and Skanda. They also live with Shiva's constant companion and *vahana* (vehicle), Nandi the bull—a symbol of male strength and power.

LORD OF THE DANCE

One of the most popular images of Shiva is as Lord of the Dance, or Shiva Nataraja. Nataraja dances within a circle representing the universe and the continual destruction and creation of life. The locks of his hair are decked with a crescent moon, a skull, and a tiny symbol of the sacred river Ganges. The skull, with its faint smile, laughs at people who consider themselves eternal, unable to realize how fleeting life is. The crescent moon in his matted hair keeps Kama, the god of nightly love, alive, and through the waxing and waning of the moon he creates different seasons and rejuvenates life.

The river Ganges that flows in Nataraja's hair originally flowed in heaven. When the heavenly Ganges was needed on earth, she was unwilling to descend because she realized that her fall from heaven would be too heavy for the earth to withstand. So Shiva, as Nataraja, agreed to break the violent power of the sacred river's fall by catching her in his tangled hair.

SNAKES, DRUM, AND FLAME

Shiva also wears snakes coiled around his upper arms and his neck, symbolizing his control over the deadliest animals. Although Hindus consider snakes the most dreaded poisonous animals on land, Shiva's power diminishes their terrible nature. Snakes also symbolize the transmigration or change that souls undergo as they inhabit different bodies. Snakes shed their skin in due season and grow a new one—just as in Hindu belief humans obtain a new body with each rebirth of their soul.

In two of his four hands Shiva often holds a drum and a flame. The drum represents the rhythmic sound to which Nataraja dances and continually recreates the universe. The flames represent the destructive energy with which Nataraja dances at the end of each cosmic age, cleansing sins and removing illusion. His right hand blesses devotees. His left hand, pointing toward his foot,

THE ELIXIR OF IMMORTALITY

One myth about Shiva, one of the three major gods of the Puranic period, tells how the gods were constantly struggling with demons (*raksasas*). To strengthen themselves in their struggle the gods decided to use *amrita,* the elixir of immortality. To produce this elixir they had to churn the Ocean of Milk. The gods used the serpent Vasuki as their churning rope. Having been churned around for some time, the serpent vomited forth poison. Just as the poison was about to fall into the elixir, contaminate it, and destroy all hope for the gods, Shiva, the god of gods, came to the rescue. He caught the poison in his mouth and saved the gods' drink of immortality. He himself was saved from swallowing it by his wife, Parvati, who strangled him so that the poison would stay in his throat. This is why some portraits of Shiva give him a blue throat.

A statue of Shiva Nataraja. Throughout the Hindu legends Shiva is depicted in many different forms. A popular form of Shiva is that of the lord of dance, Nataraja. His sacred cosmic dance has the power to remove all evils and obstacles. Nataraja stands in a posture of dance in the middle of a fiery halo. This flaming *mandorla* represents the universe with all its illusion, suffering, and pain.

grants eternal bliss to those who approach him. The other foot treads firmly upon the dwarf of ignorance, allowing the birth of knowledge.

REGENERATION AND SEXUAL POWER

In addition Shiva's form as Nataraja reveals a tradition of honoring the power of female and male sexuality. From Nataraja's left earlobe hangs a female earring and from his right earlobe a male earring. These symbolize the union of the archetypal parents of the universe.

The worship of sexual power that was so prominent in pre-Aryan times had no place in the early Vedic hymns. However the tradition of reverence for sexual power and the need for self-control was probably carried on for centuries outside the Vedas in the Brahmanic tradition. With the emergence in the *puranic* texts of both Shiva and Shakti—the primeval father and mother—the worship of sexual power resurfaced. Furthermore several of the most potent symbols in Hinduism are associated with Shiva as the god of regeneration and sexuality.

In Shaivism, which is the cult of Shiva worship, the central objects of reverence are symbols of sexual power. Even the Ultimate Reality of Brahman is often represented by symbolic forms of the genitals, such as the pillar of light and the golden egg. At times Mother Earth is referred to as the womb and Father Sky and Space as the lingam, a symbol of male sexuality. In *puranic* sacrificial rituals, the fire is called a lingam, while the yoni, or hearth, is a symbol of female sexuality. Both are common Shaivite symbols. The most commonly known lingam is the fire lingam, which is referred to as Jyotirlinga. In Hindu mythology Jyotirlinga is one of the forms of the god Shiva.

SONS OF SHIVA AND PARVATI

As Hindu mythology relates, Shiva and Parvati reside in the Himalayas with their sons, Ganesha and Skanda (who is sometimes called Kartikeya). Ganesha is an elephant-headed god, the remover of obstacles, who is invoked at the beginning of every Hindu undertaking. Skanda is an immortal warrior, the defender

A PILLAR OF FIRE

In one myth Shiva, in the form of fire as Jyotirlinga, asserts his supremacy over two other high gods, Brahma and Vishnu. The myth is told as follows:

One day Brahma noticed Vishnu, with his thousand omniscient eyes, lying on the formless waters, supported by the thousand-headed serpent of the Infinite. Impressed by Vishnu's radiance, Brahma asked the eternal being who he was. Vishnu raised his sleepy lotus eyes, smiled, and beckoned to Brahma in a condescending manner. Brahma was offended by Vishnu's informal attitude, and responded, "How can you treat me as a master would his pupil? I am the cause of creation and destruction, the creator of a thousand universes, the source of all that exists!" Vishnu replied, "Don't you know that I am Narayana, creator, preserver, and destroyer of the worlds, eternal male, immortal source of the universe, and its center as well? Even thou are born of my indestructible body."

Brahma and Vishnu thus argued bitterly above the formless sea, when a glorious, shimmering lingam appeared before their eyes. The lingam was a flamboyant pillar with the brilliance of a hundred fires, capable of consuming the universe. It was without beginning, without middle, and without end, incomparable and indescribable. Then the divine Vishnu, troubled as Brahma was by the flames, said to him, "We must look for the source of this fire. I shall go down in the form of a boar. You shall rise up in your manifestation of a swan."

"I Create, I Maintain, I Destroy"

Taking the shape of a blue boar with sharp tusks, a long snout, and firm, short feet, Vishnu plunged into the depths for a thousand years. However, despite his enduring effort, he could not find the base of the fire lingam. Meanwhile the white swan with burning eyes and great wings, whose flight was as swift as the wind, soared for a thousand years to find the top of the pillar. He too was unable to reach it. Brahma was returning when he met the great Vishnu, likewise returning, weary and disconcerted. Suddenly they saw Shiva standing before them as Jyotirlinga. They bowed before him. Vishnu said to Shiva, "Our dispute has been blessed by you, the god of gods, since you appeared before us to put an end to our argument." Shiva replied, "I am supreme lord, undivided. I am three: Brahma, Vishnu, and Shiva. I create, I maintain, I destroy."

Many different myths exist concerning the origins of Ganesha's elephant head. According to one account Parvati, before starting to bathe one day, scraped the ointment from her body and mixed it with oils and other ointments. From this she formed a man's figure and gave it life by sprinkling it with water from the Ganges River. She then set this figure, her son Ganesha, outside the bathhouse door to stand guard. When Shiva tried to enter, Ganesha refused to let him in. As Shiva did not know him, he became angry and cut off Ganesha's head. When Parvati emerged and found her son dead, she was overwrought with grief. Shiva felt sympathy for his wife, so he sent a messenger to seek another head for the child. The first creature the messenger found was an elephant. He brought back the elephant's head, and this was planted on Ganesha's shoulders.

A shrine to the elephant-headed god Ganesha.

of the gods, who is associated with Agni and Indra. Many stories are written about the two brothers.

GOD OF WISDOM AND KNOWLEDGE

Some accounts of Ganesha's origins suggest that Shiva created him in response to a request by the gods and sages, who had realized that there was no overseer of good or bad deeds. Shiva pondered over this lack of a guide for some time, then turned toward Parvati. As he looked at her a radiant youth of great beauty, endowed with the qualities of Shiva, sprang forth from his gaze. All the heavenly hosts were amazed and captivated by his beauty.

Parvati was jealous and angered by her husband's production of such a beautiful son. She cursed the son, wishing that he would become ugly and have an elephant's head. Shiva countered her curse by declaring that despite his son's elephantine head, he would be the guardian of successes and failures and would rule over all occasions. He declared that Ganesha would be great among gods, that he would be the god of wisdom and prudence, and that he would be a scribe and learned in all the scriptures. Today Ganesha is represented as a short, pot-bellied man with four arms and an elephant head.

CIRCLING THE UNIVERSE

The stories of Ganesha that have been handed down over the many centuries show the complexity of his personality. These stories point to the variety of traditions that have gone to create the complex portraits we have of Ganesha—Ganesha is a god of wisdom, he brings good luck and can remove obstacles, but he is also associated with the principles of yoga. They also show how Hinduism has been a fluid religion, even in its portraits of the ever-surviving characters that descend from Shiva.

One story of Ganesha and his brother, Kartikeya, tells how they were rivals for the same wives. To settle their dispute they agreed that whoever first circled the world would win the wife of his choosing. Kartikeya set off and after a long, wearying excur-

The "auspicious" head of Shiva shows a crescent moon, indicating the phases of lunar time. A miniature form of the sacred river Ganges adorns Shiva's matted hair. A smiling skull adorns the front of his headgear, and his dissimilar earrings represent his male and female aspects.

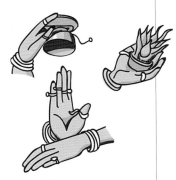

These three drawings depict three hand gestures of Shiva. In his upper left hand, he carries the drum, whose sound symbolizes the creation of the cosmos. In his upper right hand, he carries the flame, which symbolizes the simultaneous destruction of the cosmos. Shiva's lower hands are together in a gesture of blessing and reassurance.

sion, he returned home. There he found Ganesha—who had never left—already married to both young women. The elephant-headed brother explained to Kartikeya that instead of making the painstaking journey around the world, he had simply circled around their father, Shiva, who is the equivalent of the universe!

A SON TO KILL A DEMON

In some myths Kartikeya is married to Kumari. In many others he is portrayed as someone not interested in women. He rides a peacock, carries bows and arrows, and has six heads and six pairs of arms. Accounts of Kartikeya's origins and his strange appearance vary. In one very popular myth the demon Taraka was creating havoc in the heavens, and the gods discussed how they could put an end to this tyranny. They decided that they had to persuade Shiva to have a son who would kill Taraka.

Unfortunately Shiva was engaged in deep meditation. At the same time Parvati was also deeply absorbed in meditation. Shiva took no notice of her, nor she of him. Seeing this, the gods ordered Kama, the god of love, to approach Shiva, the great ascetic, and stir up a strong desire in his heart for Parvati. Kama obediently went to Mount Kailasha in the Himalayas, saw Shiva still meditating, and found beautiful Parvati now gathering flowers. Kama thought Shiva could be attracted by Parvati's beauty, so he drew his arrow and let it fly. As the arrow struck Shiva, desire awoke in his heart. However then Shiva not only saw Parvati—he also saw Kama. He realized that the god of love was trying to manipulate him. This made Shiva so angry that he burned Kama to ashes instantly.

Though desire had been aroused in his heart, Shiva, the lord of asceticism, did not give way to his passion. He consented to marry Parvati, but no children were born. Again the gods decided to take matters into their own hands. They sent Agni as their ambassador to urge Shiva to beget a son. Agni, disguised as a bird, flew around, watching Shiva constantly. Finally he managed to pick up a seed of the great god in his beak. As he flew his burden seemed to grow heavier and heavier until finally, as he was

GREAT YOGI AND TEACHER

This statue represents Shiva seated deep in meditation on top of the Himalayas. He has an antelope skin wrapped around him and snakes coiled around his neck, and he has a trident behind him. The three prongs of the trident represent the three aspects of Vishnu as creator, protector, and destroyer.

Vishnu is often depicted as a handsome young man dressed in royal robes, reclining with his wife, Lakshmi, on the coil of the serpent Ananta (or Shesha). He has four hands with which he holds a conch shell, a discus, a club, and a lotus flower. The Garuda, a creature half man and half eagle, is Vishnu's *vahana* (vehicle). Vishnu resides in a heavenly city called Vaikuntha, which is said to be made entirely of gold and precious jewels. This city is located on the mythical Mount Meru. The river Ganges, which according to some myths has its source in Vishnu's foot, flows through the city. In the pools of this heaven grow blue, red, and white lotuses. Vishnu and Lakshmi sit amid the white lotuses, where they both radiate like the sun.

A statue of Shiva at Chattapur Temple in New Delhi, India.

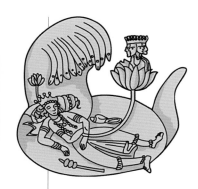

passing over the river Ganges, he was forced to drop it. There on the banks of the Ganges arose a child as beautiful as the moon and as brilliant as the sun. This was Kartikeya. As he appeared on the bank of the Ganges, six royal women came to bathe. Each of them wanted this beautiful son as her own and wished to feed him. So the newborn god acquired six mouths and was suckled by all of his foster mothers.

The beneficent god Vishnu reclines on the thousand–headed primordial serpent. From his navel emerges Brahma, the world creator. The world is ruled by Vishnu for a *yuga* (a long period of time), after which it is dissolved and re-created. Thus the cycle of *samsara* goes on.

VISHNU AND THE TEN AVATARS

In the period of the Vedas, Vishnu was a minor divinity. He was associated with the Aryan warrior god, Indra. Gradually Vishnu gained importance, and by the time of the great epics he was a paramount *deva* of the Hindu trinity: Brahma, Shiva, and Vishnu. He is known as a strong but kind god. He is a father-like figure and a just ruler. He is worshipped with great devotion and little fear. The Vaishnavites (the followers of Vishnu) worship him as the greatest of the gods, the preserver, and the ever-present spirit.

THE PRESERVER AND RESTORER

Vishnu's role as preserver seems to have developed as a means to maintain balance in the universe between good and evil powers. In the normal course of events the gods and demons are evenly matched in the world. At times, however, demons seem to gain the upper hand. During such times Vishnu, as preserver, intervenes to restore balance by descending to earth in the form of an incarnation. "Whenever the Sacred Law fails, and evil raises its head, I [Vishnu] take embodied birth. To guard the righteous, to root out sinners, and to establish the Sacred Law, I am born from age to age." (Bhagavad Gita IV.6–8)

Hindu mythology holds that there are 10 incarnations of Vishnu, called avatars. During each incarnation Vishnu has a specific task to perform.

Buddha

Traditionally the ninth avatar of Vishnu was the religious sage, the Buddha. Some Hindu texts state that Vishnu, as the Buddha, taught wrong religious ideas to evil people. Other texts claim that the Buddha was born to save innocent animals as part of his doctrine of nonviolence to all living things.

FOUR ANIMAL AVATARS

Of the 10 avatars, four are animals. In the form of Matsya (a fish), Vishnu saved the sage Manu and the sacred Vedas from a great flood. Also in this flood the gods temporarily lost the elixir of their immortality. Vishnu assumed the form of Kurma, a great tortoise, and dove to the bottom of the ocean to retrieve the potent drink.

When the demon Hiranyaksha cast the earth to the bottom of the sea, Vishnu became Varaha, the boar. He plunged into the depths, saved the earth, and spread it on top of the waters to float. Another demon, the tyrant Hiranyakashapa, had obtained a special privilege through which he could be killed neither by human nor animal, neither inside nor outside of his home, nor by day nor by night. He lived without fear and wreaked great havoc wherever he went. To overcome the demon Vishnu took the form of the Narasimha (half human and half lion) and killed Hiranyakashapa on the threshold of his home at sunset.

The Avatar Yet to Come

Vishnu's 10th avatar is the only incarnation of Vishnu that is yet to come. It is believed that this manifestation of the great god referred to as Kalki will appear at the "end" of the present time, riding a white horse and holding a flaming sword.

HUMAN AVATARS

Other avatars were human in form. A popular legend told of the three great strides with which Vishnu stepped over the universe and foiled the demon-king Bali. The demon-king had control of the earth, so Vishnu devised a plan to deceive him. Vishnu took the form of Vamana, the dwarf, and asked the king if he could have as much space as he could cover in three steps. Believing that the dwarf could only cover a small space, Bali agreed. Then Vishnu became Vamana, a great giant, and strode across the earth and the heavens. At another time the Kshatriyas (the warrior class) threatened to seize power from the Brahmins. So Vishnu was born as the Brahmin Parashurama, known as Rama with the Ax, to assert the sanctity of the caste system.

All 10 avatars were recognized in the sacred scriptures by around the 11th century C.E. By far, however, the most widely worshipped of these gods were Rama and Krishna, the seventh and eighth avatars of Vishnu.

THE ADVENTURES OF RAMA, PRINCE OF AYODHYA

Rama, the prince of Ayodhya, was the seventh avatar of Vishnu. The great epic poem the Ramayana ("Adventures of Rama") tells of Rama's life. Rama's task in this incarnation was to subdue the powerful 10-headed Ravana, demon-king of Sri Lanka. The demon-king's demise is a focal point of the Ramayana.

KING RAVANA

The king Ravana was said to be a devoted student of Vedic rituals. Brahma rewarded his devotion with a gift of invulnerability. Rav-

A huge wooden statue of the demon-king Ravana is set alight with fireworks in Manchester, England, at the end of the festival of Navaratri. In northern India events from the Ramayana are colorfully reenacted during the festival, which lasts for nine nights and culminates in the burning of Ravana.

ana could be killed neither by god nor demon. However, Ravana misused Brahma's gift; he conquered the heavens and brought all the gods to Sri Lanka, where they served him in chains. Indra became his wreath maker, Brahma his messenger, Agni his cook, Vishnu his steward, Shiva his barber, Vayu his sweeper, and Varuna his water carrier. Thus Ravana's uncompromising devotion to the god Brahma was so profound that it shook the foundations of the celestial, atmospheric, and earthly worlds.

The gods appealed to Vishnu for a solution to their predicament. Vishnu declared that Ravana had been too proud to ask for immunity from mere mortals. As a result he would be slain because of a woman, by a human, and aided by animals. Then Vishnu incarnated himself as Rama, a mere mortal and oldest son of King Dasratha who ruled from his capital, Ayodhya, in northern India.

RAMA IS SENT INTO EXILE

Rama married a princess named Sita. Shortly after the marriage Dasratha decided to retire and make his son Rama king. Dasratha's queen, however, asked the king for a favor he had promised to her long before. She asked that her son Bharata take the throne as king, and that Rama be exiled for 14 years. Dasratha was utterly disheartened, but he kept his word.

Rama wanted to go into exile alone, but his wife Sita, and his brother and best friend, Lakshmana, insisted on accompanying him. So while all of Rama's loyal subjects mourned their departure, the three companions set off into the forest. Rama's father, Dasratha, died of grief within a few days.

In the meantime Bharata was returning from a journey for what he thought was to be the coronation of his brother Rama. When he learned what had happened he was appalled. Bharata went to the forest to persuade his elder brother to return to the throne. However, Rama politely refused, saying that he could not oppose his father's word. Bharata returned to the kingdom but reigned only as a viceroy, preserving a pair of Rama's sandals on the throne as a symbol of the rightful king.

SURPANAKHA TAKES REVENGE

The demon-king Ravana's sister, Surpanakha, often visited the forest where Rama, Sita, and Lakshmana lived. She fell in love with Rama, but he resisted her advances because he loved Sita. Angered, Surpanakha turned her affections toward Lakshmana. Lakshmana ignored her completely. When she persisted he became very annoyed and cut off her nose and ears.

Surpanakha was crazed. She decided to entice her brother Ravana with details of Sita's beauty. She told him what a perfect wife Sita would be for him. Ravana was intrigued, but he was also well aware of Rama's power. Ravana knew that it would be most difficult to take Sita from Rama.

To get Sita, Ravana sent an enchanted deer to the forest. This deer was so beautiful that Sita asked Rama and Lakshmana to catch it for her. While the two brothers chased the deer, Ravana disguised himself as an ascetic. He approached Sita and took her away in his chariot to his golden palace in Sri Lanka. On the way Jatayu, Rama's bird friend, saw them. He tried to save Sita but was mortally wounded.

HANUMAN—THE MONKEY-GENERAL

Meanwhile the two brothers returned from their quest to capture the enchanted deer. They found Jatayu and learned from the wounded bird what had happened. Greatly disturbed, Rama made plans to rescue Sita. He made an alliance with the monkey-king Sugriva, who presented Rama with an army of monkeys and bears. The general of this army was the mighty Hanuman, son of Vayu, the wind god. Before anyone else could reach Sri Lanka Hanuman had flown to Ravana's palace and found Sita alone in a garden. He gave her Rama's ring as a token and assured her that Rama would rescue her. However, Hanuman was caught by Ravana's guards, who brought him before the demon-king. Ravana ordered the guards to wrap oily rags around Hanuman's tail and set fire to them. However Hanuman managed to escape, jumping from building to building with his burning tail trailing behind him. He set fire to all the buildings of the golden palace.

Because he was able to fly, Hanuman flew back to the mainland where he rejoined Rama. Upon hearing Hanuman's story Rama went to Sri Lanka with the monkey army, and a mighty battle was fought before the gates of the city. During the battle Hanuman, with golden skin, red face, and enormous tail, was terrifyingly valiant. However his greatest service was his flight to the Himalayas from which he brought herbs to heal Rama and Lakshmana when they were wounded.

RAVANA IS DEFEATED

The forces of Ravana fought vigorously, but all the demons, including Ravana's two brothers, were killed. Finally Rama and Ravana faced each other in combat. The earth trembled as they fought, and the whole company of gods watched. At one point Rama felt that Ravana had begun to overpower him. Rama drew out the dreaded *brahmastra,* a magic weapon fused with the energy of many gods. He strung the weapon on his bow and, whispering a Vedic mantra, shot it toward Ravana and killed him. At that moment all the gods showered Rama with wreaths. Rama and Sita were reunited and returned to their kingdom with Lakshmana and Hanuman.

The Ramayana tells how Hanuman, the monkey-general, lifted a mountain from the Himalayas and flew with it to Sri Lanka. The healing herbs that grew on this mountain were used to heal Rama and Lakshmana.

SITA'S EXILE

It is said that during Rama's reign the world was more peaceful than ever before. But the people of his kingdom began to gossip about Sita. They charged that because she had lived in Ravana's palace she might not be fit to be the queen. The people mistrusted Sita, so Rama felt obliged to send his queen into exile, even though she was pregnant at the time. She took refuge in a forest hermitage where she gave birth to twin sons, Luv and Kush.

When the twins were 15 years old they went to visit the capital and were recognized by their father. Rama then sent for Sita. He called together a great assembly so that Sita could publicly declare her innocence. In front of the assembly Sita called upon Earth, her mother (for Sita had been born in a furrow), to prove her innocence. The earth opened and swallowed her into its womb. Rama was heartbroken and wished to follow her. He walked into the river, where Brahma's voice welcomed him into heaven.

KRISHNA

One of Hinduism's most widely worshipped gods is Krishna, the eighth avatar of Vishnu. His popularity may be partly due to his extremely colorful character. From his childhood, Krishna performed many great feats. As a youth he dallied with milkmaids and as a young man he slayed the demon Kansa. In middle age, as a great ruler, he took part in the mythological Mahabharata War, which is described in the great epic Mahabharata.

The story of Krishna starts with the demon Kansa, a tyrant who usurped the throne of his own father, Ugrasena, and imprisoned him. Kansa had heard from a sage that a son of one of his female relatives would bring about his demise. So the demon-king ordered all her children to be slain. Immediately six children were put to death. However, her seventh child, Balarama, and her eighth child, Krishna, were miraculously saved and secretly given to foster parents. When Kansa learned of their escapes he ordered a massacre. Again the brothers were saved. Nanda and Yasoda, Krishna's foster parents, fled to Gokula and raised the boys among the milkmaids and cowherds.

The Characters of the Ramayana

For Hindus the characters of the Ramayana are models of human existence. Rama was not only a just king but an ideal son for having honored his father's promise. Sita was an ideal wife because she gave up queenly comforts to be with her husband. Lakshmana was a model brother who, like Sita, left the comforts of royalty to support Rama. Hanuman was the ideal devotee who followed and served faithfully. All of these characters are celebrated in Hindu households and frequently mentioned in Hindu sacred and secular literature.

PLAYFUL YET STRONG

In early childhood Krishna revealed a dual character. Sometimes he was a normal, lovable baby. At other times he exhibited

THE LOVE OF THE INDIVIDUAL FOR THE DIVINE

As a young man Krishna was renowned for his playful and amorous adventures with numerous maidens. One tale tells of his encounter with a hunchbacked, ugly maiden, Kubja, who was bearing perfumed oils for tyrant-demon Kansa. When Krishna asked her for some of the perfume, she rubbed it on his body. In return Krishna pressed on her feet with his own foot, lifted her chin, and straight-ened her. Other adventures with a milkmaid named Radha are told in stories noted for their beauty and sensuous descriptions. These stories also have a spiritual meaning because in them Krishna symbolizes the universal soul, and the milkmaids are individual souls longing to be united with the Ultimate Reality and achieve enlightenment.

A painting of Krishna playing his flute to the milkmaids.

extraordinary, superhuman strength. One popular myth tells of Krishna's encounter with the demon Putna, an ogress who, disguised as a beautiful girl, would suckle babies with her poisoned breasts. However her poison could not harm Krishna—he sucked so hard that he drew all the life out of Putna. The youthful Krishna often amused himself by playing pranks on his adoptive mother and the milkmaids of Gokula. He stole curds and butter, raided orchards for fruit, upset pails of milk, and blamed the other children for all his mischief.

A PLOT TO SLAY KRISHNA AND HIS BROTHER

All through Krishna's growing years Kansa continued to plot his death, but Krishna was always able to fend off the tyrant's attempts. Krishna destroyed the snake demon Kaliya by dancing on his head. He also swallowed a fire demon sent to consume the young god and his companions.

Finally the demon-king Kansa masterminded a plot to slay both Krishna and his brother Balarama. To kill them he would host a series of athletic games and invite them both. On their way to the court of Mathura, where the games would be held, Krishna and Balarama encountered many of Kansa's cohorts—demons and monsters and ogres. Krishna and Balarama thwarted these evil beings just as they did the host of gruesome demons that appeared at the games.

Finally Kansa himself opposed Krishna, only to have the prophecy of the sage come true: Krishna slew Kansa. Having done so, Krishna restored Ugrasena, the rightful king, to the throne. He also traveled to the underworld to bring back to life the six brothers who were killed at birth by Kansa. Then Krishna abandoned the pastoral life and became a feudal prince, thus entering the last phase of his life.

THE MAHABHARATA WAR

Krishna's struggles with the forces of evil climaxed in the Mahabharata War between his kinsmen, the Pandavas and the Kauravas. In a prewar council Krishna tried to reconcile the opposing parties, but to no avail. Then, since he had promised not to participate actively in the skirmish, Krishna disguised himself as the charioteer of Arjuna, a member of the Pandava family. Arjuna asked his charioteer to draw up to a point from which they could survey the battlefield. While looking down on the opposed forces of his family, Arjuna questioned the reasoning of family members killing one another.

Krishna's response to Arjuna—contained in the well-known Hindu scripture, the Bhagavad Gita—is about religious obligation and devotion to God. In his discussion Krishna informs Arjuna of the higher universal order to which he must be true—that which is beyond the temporary existence of this world. He points out that Arjuna is of the warrior caste and that he must fulfill his duty as a warrior. Krishna also tells Arjuna that though his body may die, his soul is indestructible.

> ### A Pure Soul
>
> In the Bhagavad Gita Krishna describes his relation to his devotees:
>
> *A leaf, a flower, a fruit, or water whoever offers to me with devotion—that same, proffered in devotion by one whose soul is pure, I accept.*
>
> *Even if a person of extremely vile conduct worships me being devoted to none else, he is to be reckoned as righteous, for he has engaged himself in action in the right spirit. Quickly does he become of righteous soul and obtains eternal peace. Know for certain that my devotee perishes not.*
>
> *For those who take refuge in me, even though they be lowly born, women, vaishyas (the third Hindu caste), and also sudras (the lowest Hindu caste) even they attain to the highest goal.*

THE BHAGAVAD GITA

Stories of Krishna appear in many Hindu texts, but the most well-known and respected of these are the teachings found in the Bhagavad Gita. The Bhagavad Gita is a very short section (about 18 chapters) of the 90,000 verses of the Mahabharata. Teachings in the Bhagavad Gita are revered by Hindus of many traditions. Many Hindus have memorized verses from the Gita, and often parts of the Gita are spoken during daily devotions. The teachings of the Gita, whose author is unknown, are spoken in the scripture by Krishna.

Instead of bringing out differences among the various systems of Hindu thought and practice, the Bhagavad Gita emphasizes the points of agreement among them. It thereby brings about a reli-

A guru speaking to devotees on the teachings of the Bhagavad Gita in the town of Vridavan, where Krishna lived as a child. Vridavan, its surrounding forests and the river Yamuna, which flows through the town are major Hindu sites of pilgrimage, particularly for devotees of Krishna.

gious and philosophical unity. It discusses *sva-dharma*, the individual's duties or social obligations. It stresses the significance of all the castes. Furthermore this text recommends total devotion, or bhakti, as the most effective form of religion. It assumes that there is a personal god who blesses with divine grace the devoted worshippers.

ARJUNA'S RELATIONSHIP WITH KRISHNA

Arjuna's relationship with Krishna existed on many levels. He was Krishna's warrior and student, and he was completely devoted to him. Arjuna's devotion to Krishna was intensified when Krishna revealed to him his awesome forms—as all gods, Brahman, the soul of the world.

The relationship Arjuna had with Krishna is an example of an individual having a personal god. This kind of relationship is further elaborated by poet-sages throughout India from the eighth to the 16th century. These writers have produced widely popular literature.

There are various stories about the details of the last days of Krishna and Balarama but, following the Mahabharata War, Balarama died in his sleep and departed from this world. Krishna mourned alone for some time then ascended to heaven.

THE SUPREME GODDESS MAHADEVI SHAKTI

Goddesses have been revered since the pre-Aryan time of the Indus Valley culture, when devotees attributed the fertility of the land to a maternal deity. By the Vedic period significant female deities had emerged. These include Prithvi, the earth goddess, and Vac, the goddess of speech and wisdom.

In the epics the consorts—Sarasvati, Parvati, and Lakshmi— of the three major gods had become quite prominent in themselves. Sarasvati (associated with Vac) is regarded as the goddess of all the creative arts, sciences, and knowledge. Parvati, the wife of Shiva, is associated with the Himalayas. Like her husband she has immense ascetic and erotic characteristics. Lakshmi, Vishnu's consort, is associated with the lotus, symbol of power and good luck.

MANIFESTATIONS OF ONE GODDESS

Though these goddesses came to hold much respect in the minds of goddess devotees, the great goddess Mahadevi Shakti is the one ultimate reality. In addition to the three major goddesses, numerous minor goddesses are revered by Hindus. However, all the goddesses are manifes-

Father of the Universe

The Bhagavad Gita tells how Arjuna's chief feelings for Krishna were awe inspired:

*You (Krishna) are the father
of the universe,
of all that moves and all that moves not,
its worshipful and worthy teacher.
You have no equal—what in the
three worlds
could equal you O power
beyond compare?*

*So, reverently prostrating my body,
I crave your grace, O blessed lord
As father to son, as friend to friend,
as lover to beloved, bear with me, god.*

tations of Mahadevi, the great goddess. With the popularity of the sixth-century Markandya Purana, worship of the great goddess had become well established. At present goddess worship is visible primarily in the villages, and many of these goddesses have only local reputations. In the minds of villagers all these local goddesses are associated with the great goddess, Mahadevi Shakti.

DEVOTED AND DESTRUCTIVE ASPECTS

Mahadevi is an active and powerful female who is attentive to the stability of the world and to the needs of her devotees. She is worshipped for her different aspects, including those of the great maternal goddess and the devoted consort or wife. Her character has a beneficent side as well as a destructive side. Hindus perceive the two sides of Mahadevi as a natural part of an orderly universe containing both positive and negative forces—life and death, creation and destruction, vigor and rest.

In her fierce form the great goddess is Durga. Durga was created out of angry flames that issued forth from the mouths of Brahma, Vishnu, Shiva, and other gods. She was specifically created by the gods to kill the buffalo demon Mahisha, who by abstinence had gained the strength to drive the gods from their celestial kingdom.

Durga was born fully grown and beautiful, riding a tiger from the Himalayan forests. She was immediately armed by the gods, and in each of her 10 hands she held special weapons: Vishnu's discus, Shiva's trident (three-pronged spear), Agni's flaming dart, Indra's thunderbolt, and Varuna's conch shell, among others. With these weapons Durga killed the buffalo-demon and returned the gods to their rightful kingdom.

MILD AND FIERCE FORMS OF MAHADEVI SHAKTI

The complexity of the great goddess Mahadevi Shakti—in such forms as Sati, Parvati, Durga, and Kali—is expressed in a variety of roles that she shares with her husband, Shiva. She is both mild and fierce. In her mild form she is Sati, daughter of a sage who marries Shiva against her father's wishes. Later she sacrifices herself on her father's sacrificial fire because he does not approve of Shiva, her husband. After some time Sati is reborn as Parvati, the daughter of Himavat, god of mountains. She practices austere yoga. Shiva is impressed by her yogic powers and marries her again.

DEFEATING THE DEMON BROTHERS

On another occasion the gods appealed to the goddess Durga to eliminate the demon brothers Sumbha and Nisumbha. Shiva had blessed the brothers with immortality because they had performed acts that made the gods tremble. As a goddess capable of defeating demons, Durga agreed to combat the brothers. When she appeared before Sumbha his passion was aroused, and he desired to possess her. She agreed to consent only if he could overcome her in battle. Sumbha accepted the condition unhesitatingly, not realizing that the immortality granted him was protection from gods only, and not from goddesses. And so Durga defeated the demon and his brother with ease.

Despite her grace Durga combated many demons who had received benefits that protected them from gods and men. Her primary role was to maintain and protect cosmic order by appearing periodically to battle such demon oppressors.

KALI—"THE BLACK ONE"

Kali, "the black one," personifies the most terrifying aspects of Mahadevi Shakti. She leaves bloodshed, disease, and death in her wake. One myth tells of how Kali rid the world of the dreaded tyrant Raktabija. Wherever a drop of his blood fell thousands of demons would appear. Thus Kali slew him and drained all the blood from his body.

With all her gruesome characteristics, Kali became an ultimate representation of death. Many Hindus believe that spiritual enlightenment can be achieved if the terrifying aspects of this deity, the image of all life's fear and pain, can be overcome.

Through centuries of change in customs and traditions a growing pantheon of Hindu goddesses and gods represent a range of beliefs. However, the various groups did have one common goal: They wanted to perceive the Supreme power behind the various deities on a more personal level than had previously been thought possible. This desire grew in popularity and blossomed into an influential movement based on personal devotion to an individual deity.

KALI

Kali is the most frightening form of Mahadevi Shakti, Her body is usually decked with terrible ornaments made from bones; a string of human skulls adorns her neck. She wields a sword in one hand, a dagger in another, and the severed heads of two giants hang, dripping blood, from her two other hands. Her hair is wildly disheveled, tusks protrude from her face, a third eye peers out from the middle of her forehead, and she is often portrayed with her tongue hanging out. Having overcome the power of death, she dwells in the cremation ground, seating herself on corpses.

A shrine to Kali in the courtyard of a temple in Kathmandu, Nepal.

BHAKTI, OR DEVOTION

The most important theme throughout the epics and the *puranas* was that of bhakti, or devotion. Early bhakti reflected the cultural and social changes that were taking place in Hindu society before and during Islamic rule. The bhakti movement was very different from traditionally Vedic-based ceremonies and attitudes, although the authority of the Vedas was never renounced. More recent religious texts stress the independence of bhakti religion from other means of salvation.

PURITY OF HEART, POVERTY, AND COMPASSION

Bhakti was conceived as a way of life, a selfless and complete surrender to God. Members of the movement invoked their goddess or god by name and recited hymns of praise, always being mindful of the deity. Devotees were to acknowledge no difference between themselves and others. They were required to be free of jealousy, falsehood, envy, and injury. Bhakti devotees were discouraged from taking pride in their birthright or wealth. The teachings of bhakti implied that a person's birth and caste had no significant influence on their salvation—salvation depended only on a devotee's purity of heart.

The teachings also carried over into social attitudes. Material poverty was looked on with favor. Great compassion was shown for the persecuted, distressed, and despised. And caste distinctions were declared irrelevant. Women have not only played significant roles in the Hindu tradition as mothers and wives, they also have magnificently contributed to various other fields of life. In the area of religion two women who come to mind are the saint-poetesses of the bhakti movement: Lalleshwari (14th century) and Mira Bhai (16th century).

LITERATURE OF THE BHAKTI MOVEMENT

The writers of the bhakti movement (eighth to 17th centuries) chose to write in languages spoken by the common people of local regions. This was because Sanskrit, the language of the *puranas*, was only taught to the learned of the Brahmin caste. Sanskrit was the language of the elite, even though in earlier times it contained some popular expressions that may have come from some less educated people. The bhakti writers chose not to write in Sanskrit, to make their literature more accessible.

Intense devotional fervor was evident in the poetry of the movement. The poets produced thousands of poems in various regional languages. The poets belonged to

THE LANGUAGE OF HUMAN EMOTION

In the bhakti movement, the language of devotion was the language of human emotion, at times so intense that it was painful, highly moving, and intensely personal. The poet-sages related their relationship with God in terms of love, friendship, despair, and joy. They implied that the goal of bhakti was salvation in very personal terms, not merely an ambiguous union with the impersonal Brahman (Universal Soul). Salvation through bhakti included an eternal relationship of blissful devotion. In this relationship, unlike that pictured by the earlier ascetics, the devotee and the Ultimate Reality would remain separate. In the words of one poet, devotion was "to taste sugar, not become sugar."

UNION OF MIND AND SOUL

Poets who possessed outstanding powers of expression became quite popular all over India. An eighth-century poet from the south of India wrote:

I am false, my heart is false, my love is false,
But I, this sinner, can win thee if I weep before thee, O lord,
Thou who art sweet like
honey, nectar, and the juice of sugar cane!
Please bless me so that I can reach thee.

Lalleshwari, the 14th-century Kashmiri devotional poetess, wrote in opposition to temple worship:

Image is of stone, temple is of stone,
Above and Below are
one, which of them will you worship, O foolish Pandit?
Because within you lies the union of mind and soul.

She mocked religious persecution and discrimination, saying:

Shiva permeates this Universe
Do not discriminate between a Hindu and a Muslim
If thou art sharp enough, know thyself.

Some have abandoned home
some the forest abode
What use the hermitage if thou controllest not thine mind.

the people and integrated them by conveying this religious movement from region to region. Though they themselves were from different social levels of Hindu society, the poets helped keep Brahmanism alive. They constantly revitalized, reinterpreted, and rejuvenated Hindu ideas and beliefs, making this religion available to all people.

Basavanna, a 12th-century devotional poet from southern India, offered his body to his personal god because, unlike the rich, he could not afford to build a temple. In this poem the poet's body is compared with a temple. Basavanna reminds us that the temple has become a meaningless monument or building with its original symbolism forgotten. By identifying his body with a temple, the poet makes his body sacred, and he offers himself to God. Basavanna emphasizes that rich people only make temples, but poor people themselves become temples, exhibiting the intensity and purity of their devotion to Hinduism.

The rich
will make temples for Shiva
What shall I,
a poor man do?
My legs are pillars,
the body the shrine,
the head a cupola of gold.
Listen, O Lord,
things standing shall fall,
but the moving ever shall stay.

THE VEDANTA SUTRAS

The Vedanta Sutras were compiled in Sanskrit by Badarayana early in the first millennium. *Vedanta* literally means "the end of knowledge," and the sutras summarize the essential teachings of the Vedas and Upanishads. Each sutra is a short self-contained philosophical statement that leads to the next. The opening sutra sets the subject for the first chapter: "Now is the time to inquire into the nature of Brahman."

The second sutra follows this inquiry by supplying a definition of Brahman, the Highest Truth, as being "the source of all that is." The third sutra asserts that the Truth is to be known by studying scripture, namely the Upanishads and Vedas.

The sutras were arranged in four chapters, the first dealing with Brahman, the second the relationship between the self and Brahman, the third the way to realize Brahman, and the fourth the path to *moksha,* liberation, and oneness with Brahman. The sutras relied on the principal Upanishads and provided a systematic way to study them. Generations of students learned the sutras by heart.

SHANKARA AND RAMANUJA

Shankara (788–820) was born in Kerala, southern India. He wrote his famous commentary on the Vedanta Sutras and established the school of Advaita Vedanta, which emphasized the oneness of all reality in Brahman. He also wrote a famous commentary on the Bhagavad Gita and recognized it as the most accessible introduction to the teachings of Vedanta and yoga. Shankara established four great monasteries in different parts of India and did much to restore Vedic teachings following the spread of Buddhism.

Ramanuja (1017–1137) was the first of a succession of Vaishnava teachers who established teaching lineages and emphasized devotion. He traveled and taught all over India, and interpreted Vedanta in a theistic sense, teaching the oneness of all things in Brahman, combined with devotion to a personal deity. The great temple where he taught at Srirangam in southern India is still one of India's most popular places of worship. He too wrote an important commentary on the Bhagavad Gita, which emphasized its teaching of bhakti yoga and devotion to Krishna.

THE ESSENTIAL GUIDEBOOK

Krishna devotees, including many from the North America and Europe, chanting and offering *puja* to Krishna in a temple in Vrindavan, northern India.

The Bhagavad Gita, through these and other great teachers, became the essential guidebook that united all followers of the Vedas. It taught about the eternal self and the path to inner peace. It stressed *karma yoga*, work without attachment for the results, as the way to liberation, and devotion to Krishna as the goal of life.

REVIVAL UNDER CHAITANYA

Chaitanya (1486–1534) was born in Bengal at a time of Muslim dominance. From a young age he led a popular revival of the Vaishnava tradition based on devotion to Krishna. His special appeal was to the masses and he emphasized the simple path of chanting Krishna's names and hearing the Srimad Bhagavatam, the scripture that preserves the Vaishnava teachings and tells in poetic detail the stories of Krishna and the avatars of Vishnu. The Krishna devotees who spread around the world in the late 20th century, chanting "Hare Krishna" in the streets, were followers of Chaitanya.

It was because of devout saints that all the Hindu religious sects were woven together in a complex system. However, political integration did not follow social and cultural integration. In 712 C.E., a 21-year-old Arab military leader named Muhammad ibn Kasim swept into the Indus Valley, introducing the challenge of Islam and eras of change that would alter the face of Hinduism forever.

CHAPTER 5

POLITICAL AND SOCIAL CHANGE

The eighth century C.E. brought the beginning of an endless series of changes and challenges to India and to Hinduism. With new religions, new rulers, new laws, and new saints Hinduism proved to be a stable and flexible religious way of life.

ISLAM IN INDIA

Islam came to India first as a religion, then as a political force. In the eighth century Arabs infiltrated the Indian continent. Almost three centuries later the Afghans, the Turks, and the Persians, all Muslims, came to conquer and stayed as the rulers. By the 13th century Muslim rule had blossomed throughout most of northern India. The cultural and the political center of the new rulers was Delhi.

The Islamic culture in India reached its height under the Mughal Empire. The Mughal dynasty was founded by an Afghan warrior chief of Mongol descent named Babur in the early 16th century. The empire reached its apex of brilliance during the

Mahatma Gandhi surrounded by members of his family. Gandhi became a leading figure in India's nationalist movement working toward independence from British rule. Drawing on his Hindu beliefs, Gandhi advocated a policy of nonviolent social action.

THE POETRY OF KABIR

One of the most popular poet-sages of the Mughal period was Kabir (d. 1518). Raised a Muslim, Kabir was influenced by Sufism and later embraced Hinduism. His teachings emphasized love of God and the idea that God would return that love despite caste and creed. Kabir's writings convey the simple nature of devotional worship:

I do not ring the temple bell,
I do not set the idol on its throne,
I do not worship the image with flowers
It is not the austerities that mortify
  the flesh which are pleasing to the lord,
When you leave off your clothes and kill
  your senses, you do not please the lord.
The man who is kind and who practices
  righteousness,
who remains passive amidst the affairs
  of the world,
who considers all creatures on earth as
  his own self,
He attains the Immortal Being, the
  true God is ever with him.

reign of Babur's great-grandson Akbar the Great (r. 1556–1605). By the beginning of the 18th century, however, it had declined.

Muslim rulers dominated India for almost nine centuries. Hindus responded to this domination in a variety of ways. Some converted to Islam, but the majority remained loyal to their religious heritage. Life was difficult for Hindus under Muslim rule. Muslim rulers imposed a special tax on non-Muslims. In addition they demolished Hindu temples and destroyed countless images. The Muslims considered the Hindus to be pagans, and they especially despised the Hindu tradition of image worship. As a result an enduring hostility arose between the two groups.

For the most part Hindus and Muslims did not interact. However, poet-sages of the era drew on both religions, and Muslims supported scholars and artists, among whom Hindus numbered significantly. As a result Hinduism was influenced by Islam, and Islam by Hinduism. Some influences were more direct. The Muslims stifled the elitist Brahmanic traditions but allowed devotional movements such as bhakti to flourish. Islamic mysticism, or Sufism, had much in common with the Hindu bhakti movement. Both emphasized a direct personal relationship with God. Together they produced a religious view that supported moving away from organized sects and orthodox scriptures, toward devotional worship.

By the time the Mughal emperor Akbar came to power in the 16th century there was an active sea route between Europe and India. In the 1540s Saint Francis Xavier founded a Christian mission on Indian shores. The priests tried to convert Akbar, who became curious not only about Christianity but other religions as well. He tried to introduce religious tolerance, for example, by abolishing the special tax all non-Muslims had to pay. Akbar's successor, however, reimposed the tax and devastated many Hindu temples.

BRITISH RULE

By 1700 the Mughal Empire was in decline. By this time India's coasts were dotted with European trading settlements and missionary centers. The British moved to protect their interests in India by establishing colonies. Within 50 years the British East India Company had gained control over India's most prosperous provinces. By 1818 the British were in control of the entire Indian subcontinent, including present-day India, Pakistan, Bangladesh, and Sri Lanka.

Chatrapati Shivaji train terminus, formerly Victoria Terminal, built during the time of British rule in India. By 1818 the British were in control of the entire Indian subcontinent. During the time of the British Raj extensive administrative and transportation networks were established throughout India.

CHANGES TO HINDU LIFE

British rule brought enormous changes in Indian life. The British introduced Western education so that increasing numbers of people became literate. Occupations formerly reserved for one caste or class became open to all. Secular laws diminished the authority of the Hindu religious code. British rule thus disrupted and changed some of the basic ideas of Hinduism. It also altered the society in which Hindus had lived. Jobs in industry and business moved people to the cities. Many people found themselves free of traditional family-centered religious and social obligations they had taken for granted.

At the beginning of British rule the Indian population spoke 14 different literary languages and hundreds of dialects. British officials moved quickly to make English the dominant language in the schools and colleges. Public education was suddenly open to all. Christian missionaries came to India and opened schools

A medical student in a laboratory in a nursing college in Kerala, India. Schools, higher-education institutions, and universities are widespread throughout India. Although the number of women in higher education is not as high as that of men, it is growing every year.

and colleges for both women and men. Christianity challenged Hindu customs that had existed for centuries.

One such custom was the caste system, which justified hereditary occupations and unequal distribution of opportunities. Hindus considered the caste system to be part of the normal course of life. The miserable conditions of the lower classes were also considered normal. Women suffered under harsh codes that forced them into marriage as young girls and denied remarriage to widows, no matter how young they were. The practice of suttee required a wife to burn herself to death on the funeral pyre of her husband.

THE GROWTH OF NATIONALISM

As a result of Western influence many Indians began to doubt the traditions of Hinduism. Educated Hindus became uncomfortable with their religion after comparing it to the ethical standards of the Western countries. At the same time, however, European scholars were researching India's forgotten past. They uncovered records of a greater pre-Islamic India in which brilliant systems of thought were developed and great works of literature and art were created. Hindu religious leaders called on young people to identify with that ancient heritage and its rich cultural and spiritual resources.

Consequently, by the end of the 19th century a passionate nationalism with religious overtones began to grow in the minds of educated Indians. While recognizing that the Western countries led in science and technology, they had come to see the East as the world's center of spiritual culture. A number of prominent Hindu figures emerged at this time to lead their religion into reform.

HINDU SCHOLARS AND REFORMERS

Rammohan Roy (1772–1833) is called the father of modern India. Born of devout Brahmin parents in Bengal, he showed an intense interest in religion from his early years. He studied the Upanishadic scriptures, which he considered the core of Hinduism. Roy joined the British civil service and rose as high as was possible for an Indian at the time. He retired at 42 and settled in Kolkata (Calcutta), then the political and intellectual capital of India.

As a young man Roy had witnessed the death of his sister-in-law in the act of suttee. She was forced onto her husband's funeral pyre and held there with long poles while the sound of drums drowned out her screams. Horrified by this experience, Roy became a vehement opponent of suttee. He founded several newspapers, which he published in different languages. He campaigned against suttee, child marriage, image worship, and other Hindu customs he felt were misguided. Roy denounced polytheism, the worship of many gods. He founded a religious society, Brahmo Samaj (Society of God). Its members gathered weekly for congregational-style meetings in which people prayed, sang hymns, and listened to sermons based on the Hindu scriptures.

RAMAKRISHNA (1836–1886)

Ramakrishna was the son of a village priest. From the age of seven he experienced mystic trances and divine visions. He often meditated before the image of Kali, the great mother goddess in her terrible form, imagining that she was breathing and listening to him. One day, he believed the goddess revealed herself to him. From that time on her image or the sound of her name would send him into a trance.

Ramakrishna became an ascetic, devoting himself to prayer and meditation. Later he became a meditating yogi. He worshipped like a bhakti devotee and explored Buddhism and Shaktism (worship of the goddess Shakti).

Ramakrishna came to believe that all religions were glorifications of the same entity. He studied Islam and meditated on Muhammad until Muhammad appeared to him in a vision. Then he read the Bible and meditated on pictures of the Madonna and Child until a vision of Christ appeared to him. He declared that all religions were equally effective ways of coming into contact with divinity.

In the last years of his life Ramakrishna gathered a group of disciples around him. One of these was a young law student, Vivekananda, who became his successor.

VIVEKANANDA (1863–1902)

Vivekananda was planning to study law in England when he met Ramakrishna. He abandoned his plans for a legal career and became an ascetic. In 1893 he traveled to Chicago for the Parliament of Religions, where he spoke for Hinduism. There he declared, "All religions are one." Vivekananda traveled in America and England before returning to India, where he devoted the rest of his life to helping the poor and to religious education. His greatest achievement was that of reviving interest in Hinduism throughout the world.

RABINDRANATH TAGORE (1861–1941)

Rabindranath Tagore was the 14th of the 15 children of Debendranath Tagore, the leader of the Brahmo Samaj, one of many reform movements created in the mid-19th century. Tagore began writing poetry at 13, and at 20 he published his first volume of Bengali poems. Over the next 30 years, as he continued to write poetry, his writing matured in style and deepened in content. In 1912 Tagore published *Gitanjali* ("Song Offering") following the deaths of his wife and three of his five children. A year later he received the Nobel Prize in Literature, awarded each year to only one writer as a tribute to that writer's lifetime achievement and considered the highest honor a writer can receive.

Tagore founded a school at Shantiniketan, Bengal, for creative and performing artists. In 1921 he expanded his retreat into a university, which he dedicated to his ideal of world brotherhood and cultural

TAGORE AND GANDHI

One contemporary of the poet Rabindranath Tagore was Mohandas Gandhi, who was attaining widespread recognition as head of a movement to oppose everything British. Tagore disagreed strongly with Gandhi and his methods. He felt that politics distracted people from more important issues, such as erasing caste barriers, uplifting the poor and helpless, and reconciling Hindus and Muslims. However despite their ideological differences Rabindranath Tagore recognized Gandhi's greatness. It was he who first called Gandhi Mahatma, an honorary title meaning "the Great Soul."

Rabindranath Tagore and Mahatma Gandhi photographed in 1940.

exchange. Tagore felt that nationalism and materialism were great evils. He believed that the best hope for humanity was to return to the spiritual values found in all religions. Tagore saw India as the spiritual teacher of the world, but he valued the West's vitality and search for truth.

MOHANDAS GANDHI (1869–1948) AND THE INDIAN NATIONAL MOVEMENT

India had been under British rule for almost half a century when Mohandas Gandhi was born in 1869. Gandhi grew up in a traditional middle-class Hindu family. At 19 he went to London to study law, returning to India in 1891. Shy and reserved, he found little success in the practice of law. In 1893 he accepted a job offer in South Africa. There he experienced firsthand the prejudices held by white South Africans against Indians.

Gandhi's law job in South Africa ended after one year, but for the next 21 years he remained there working for Indian rights.

Drawing on his fundamental Hindu beliefs, he developed what he called *satyagraha*—nonviolent social action. *Satyagraha* was based on Hindu principles of truth, nonviolence, and courage. Gandhi taught that the practice of *satyagraha* in the face of injustice would bring about social change.

Gandhi returned to India in 1915. There he became leader of the Indian nationalist movement, which aimed at freeing India from British rule. Gandhi set up training centers at which he taught *satyagraha* and also life skills to help India's downtrodden poor to become self-sufficient. He renounced worldly life and possessions and devoted himself wholly to moving India toward independence. He led non-violent uprisings against British rule, even going to prison for his beliefs. Many people believed that Gandhi was divinely inspired; others came to see him as the god Vishnu returned. Rabindranath Tagore was the first to call him *Mahatma,* meaning "great soul." With great moral and political power on his side, Gandhi and his followers overcame Britain's hold on the country, and Britain agreed to withdraw from India. On August 15, 1947, India became independent.

PARTITION

The end of British rule had its costs, however. For many years an uneasy political situation had existed between the Hindus, mostly concentrated in the south and the west, and the Muslims to the north. The two groups had not only different religious views but also different social and political aims. Each mistrusted the other. Under the British they were held together by their mutual struggle against foreign domination. With independence on the horizon their differences became even more pronounced. Although the British wanted to maintain India as one country with different self-governing regions, they also suggested that if the Hindus and Muslims could not agree, they might separate into two different countries. The British would leave it up to the people to decide.

In 1947 India was partitioned and the new nation of Pakistan was created. Gandhi had hoped to maintain India as one country, but with thousands of people fleeing angry mobs, this man of conscience threw his considerable political weight behind dividing the country. He began a fast in order to draw the consciousness of the Indian people toward the plight of the Muslims. He appealed to Indians to replace hatred with love. At one of his prayer meetings in 1948, Gandhi was assassinated by a young Hindu extremist who felt that the country should not have been divided.

GANDHI'S SUCCESSORS

Gandhi left behind a double legacy. One was his commitment to *satyagraha*, the belief that truth and nonviolence could solve human problems. In this movement he was succeeded by Vinoba Bhave (1895–1970), who had worked beside him at Gandhi's ashram (religious community). Bhave became Gandhi's heir to the theory and practice of nonviolence. Beginning in 1951 Bhave persuaded rich landowners to donate more than 4 million acres of land, which he distributed to farmers to help them become self-sufficient.

In the political realm Gandhi's successor was Jawaharlal Nehru (1889–1964). Nehru had been an ally of Gandhi's in the battle for Indian independence and became the new country's first prime minister, a position that he held until 1964. Nehru's daughter, Indira, later became India's first and so far only woman prime minister.

Gandhi's influence was to continue long after his death and beyond India. In the United States in the 1960s, a young Baptist minister named Martin Luther King Jr. studied Gandhi's life and philosophy. He was particularly interested in the use of nonviolence to bring about social reform. King was later to base his strategy of nonviolent protests against segregation on Gandhi's principle of *satyagraha*.

Muslim refugees leaving New Delhi for Pakistan at Partition. When Pakistan was created and the British withdrew from India, uprisings broke out all over India. Many thousands of people died and several million more became refugees in their own country. In the end there were two new nations: India, with its heavily Hindu population, and Pakistan, which instantly became a Muslim majority state.

THE LEGACY OF REFORM

The modern leaders of Hinduism, from Rammohan Roy to Mahatma Gandhi, had a profound influence on the religion and on Indian culture. They did much to reform the internal abuses that had crept into the religion over centuries. Due to their efforts the government outlawed practices such as child marriage, suttee, and caste-based discrimination. Although old attitudes die slowly and members of lower castes still face prejudice, it is a measure of how far India and Hinduism have come that in 1997 a Dalit ("untouchable"), Kocheril Raman Narayanan, was elected president. Lower-caste members hailed his election as a major victory.

Narayanan's victory also demonstrated Hinduism's ability to adapt to changing times. In Hinduism there has always been room for change. Because of the open-ended nature of the religion saints continue to appear, and there is constant discussion and revision. Old traditions are revitalized and, if need be, new ideas are integrated and new religious societies begun. Freedom of individual thought has been intrinsically sacred to Hinduism and makes innovations possible.

The Concerns of the Common Man

In 1997 Kocheril Raman Narayanan, a Hindu from the Dalit or "untouchable" caste, was sworn in as president of India. In his address at his swearing-in ceremony Narayanan said, "That the nation has found a consensus for its highest office in someone who has sprung from the grass roots of our society . . . is symbolic of the fact that the concerns of the common man have now moved to the center stage of our social and political life."

THE RISE OF HINDU NATIONALISM

India is a deeply religious society, with indigenous religious and cultural traditions that go back many centuries. The modern Indian state, however, is fairly recent. Founded on democratic principles, the government of India is officially secular, that is, not linked to any specific religion. Religious minorities, which include Muslims, Sikhs, Parsis, and Christians, are supposed to be treated equally with Hindus. However secularism has never been very successful in this deeply spiritual land, where Hinduism is more than a religion. It is a culture and a way of life as well. More-

Hindu nationalism is built around the concept of *Hindutva*, or "Hindu-ness." For Hindu nationalists Hinduism and nationalism are so closely linked as to be the same thing. An early Hindu nationalist put it like this: "A Hindu is a person who regards this land of Bharat Varsha, from the Indus to the Seas, as his Fatherland as well as his holy land that is the cradle of his religion." According to the movement the Indian nation can only become strong through a return to its cultural roots. Nationalists define these roots as an ancient Hindu past.

Hindu nationalists feel that it is important to protect their religious and cultural traditions from secularism, which they see as an import from Western cultures and not native to India. They believe that India's religious tradition is a necessary ingredient of an Indian nation.

over, Hindus have never lost their mistrust of Muslims. Instead it has grown stronger. Their feelings have led them to define themselves in opposition to "others" and to seek a deeply and uniquely Hindu identity for themselves and for their nation.

Increasingly the notion of what it means to be Indian has come to mean "Hindu." In part a reaction to secularism, Hindu nationalism has been on the rise since well before independence. The seeds of Hindu nationalism were sown in reform movements that urged followers to turn their backs on modernity, secularism, and other outside influences and to return to the pure Hinduism of their ancestors.

HINDU NATIONALIST MOVEMENTS

The Rashtriya Swayamsevak Sangh, or RSS, is a Hindu reform movement that began in the late 19th century. It started as an organization of Hindu youth with a program that included both physical exercise and moral development. From the 1940s it has grown to become the most powerful and important Hindu nationalist organization in India.

The RSS teaches that for a nation to be successful it must have certain "unities." These are defined as geographical unity, racial unity, religious unity, cultural unity, and unity of language. The RSS argues that the Hindus fulfilled these qualifications and were the true citizens of India. Muslims may be true citizens as well but only if they recognize the essential Hinduness of the country.

During the struggle for independence the RSS appealed to young people who felt that Gandhi's *satyagraha* approach was too passive and gave away too much to minorities, particularly Muslims, as well as Christians and Sikhs. The government banned the

RSS after the riots that lead to partition in 1948, but in 1950 the organization was reinstated and continued to gather strength. It was banned again in the early 1990s for encouraging violence against ethnic minorities, but its influence had spread so widely that the ban could not have much effect.

Another important organization moving the country toward Hindu nationalism is the Vishwa Hindu Parishad, or VHP, an organization of religious leaders. These two organizations work to place Hinduism in the front of Indian life and thought.

HINDUISM AND POLITICS: THE BJP

One way that the RSS influences daily life today is through the Bharatiya Janata Party, or BJP. Many BJP leaders came out of the RSS and have links to the VHP as well. The political goals of the BJP are frankly in harmony with those of the nationalist organizations.

Although successful in the elections of 1996 and 1998, when the BJP gained the highest number of seats but not a majority in parliament, and eventually were able to put together a coalition government, the loss in the elections of 2004 left the party searching for new leaders. During the years when the BJP led the government it quite often put on the back burner issues related to Hindu nationalism and centered attention on economic reforms and development. It also tried to attract Muslim workers to its ranks; however, many of them abandoned the party after the 2004 elections.

Even though the BJP did not push for Hindu nationalism during its reign, a large number of fundamentalist Hindus did. These fundamentalists used the official declarations of the BJP to promote communalism or the deliberate creation of conflicts between religious minorities, such as the Christians and Muslims, and the majority Hindu community. The Congress government that assumed power in May 2004, with Manmohan Singh, a Sikh, as the prime minister, was more successful at focusing attention on economic reforms. As a former financial minister of India, Singh reenergized much of India's economy rather than

Separatist Movements

Kashmir is not the only part of India in which ethnic and religious minorities have rebelled against the Indian government. To the south Tamil separatists, who are mostly Buddhist, continue to create unrest. The Punjab, the cradle of the Sikh religion, was divided by partition and some Sikh separatists continue to agitate for a united and independent Sikh state. Both Christians and Sikhs blame the Hindu majority for human-rights violations.

HINDUISM IN NEPAL

To the north of India is its neighbor Nepal. By its 1962 and 1990 constitutions Nepal was a Hindu kingdom, the only one in the world. The constitution guaranteed religious freedom and forbade the state to discriminate among citizens on grounds of religion. Since about 89 percent of Nepal's citizens are Hindus, this was a great experiment in religious toleration. However, in spring 2008, following near–civil war between Marxists and the royal government under an unpopular king, the constitution was rewritten. Following an election, the monarchy was abolished and a democratic republic established. This brought an end to Nepal's status as an official Hindu kingdom, as the king was believed to be an incarnation of Vishnu.

handing leadership over to private groups of investors. The emphasis shifted to economic growth rather than any push for Hindu nationalism.

PROBLEMS OF HINDU NATIONALISM

One of the problems Hindu nationalism has faced is that by promoting Hindu values it has tended to harden the positions of its non-Hindu neighbors against it. Muslim Pakistan views opposition to Hindu India as a holy cause and has supported the uprisings in Kashmir, an Indian state in which Hindus are in the minority. The problems in Kashmir go back to partition.

Although the population was overwhelmingly Muslim, Kashmir had a Hindu ruler. Under the partition agreement Kashmir could have become part of either Pakistan or India, or it could have remained independent. When Pakistani troops invaded Kashmir to force its ruler to join Pakistan, he instead called on India for military protection and the area became Indian. Kashmir's population remains mainly Muslim, and Hindus are under almost constant attack there. Many Hindus traveling to shrines in Kashmir have died at the hands of Kashmiri rebels.

On the world stage the BJP ushered India into the nuclear age in 1998 by testing atomic bombs meant as a threat to Islamic Pakistan. Pakistan retaliated by testing nuclear weapons of its own. The age-old hostilities of the Hindus and Muslims thereby took a new and more perilous turn. In 2007 and 2008, the blame for various terrorist attacks in Hindu India has been firmly laid on Muslims trained in Pakistan.

The tension between India as a land of diverse faiths and India as the homeland of the Vedas is one that is unlikely to be resolved. Attempts to enforce Vedic—more specifically Hindu values—will be attractive to many people who feel left behind in the economic progress of India, which is so pronounced at the moment. This, combined with the slow erosion of tribal cultures under pressure from Hindu influences who often find themselves in competition with Muslim or Christian or Buddhist missionaries, will continue to be a flash point. It remains to be seen how India as a secular country will maintain this delicate balance.

CHAPTER 6

THE HINDU TEMPLE, ICONS, AND WORSHIP

The Hindu temple is known by many different names, three of which are *mandira* ("waiting place"), *prasada* ("seat of grace"), and *devalaya* ("house of God"). The most popular term for the Hindu temple is *mandira* (or *mandir*). The *mandira* is believed to be the earthly seat of a deity and the place where deities wait for their devotees. The belief that goddesses and gods dwell in the *mandira* can be traced as far back as the epics and the *puranas*.

In later sacred texts, such as the Shastras, special chapters were written about the building of a *mandira*. In these texts the *mandira* is described as a crossing place where worlds of divinity and humanity meet. Hindus believe that a deity descends to earth and takes form through sacred images located in the *mandira*. Some believe that by seeing (*darsana*) and touching the image, it is possible to ascend temporarily to heaven and experience the divine. Although Hindus believe that God is found everywhere in the world, they also have great respect for a divine world. The architectural and religious symbolism found throughout the *mandira*

Hindus on pilgrimage in the city of Varanasi, northern India. Many Hindus come to Varanasi to bathe in the waters of the sacred river Ganges. The dead are also cremated on the ghats, or steps at the water's edge, and the ashes spread on the Ganges.

helps give shape to a divine reality that would otherwise remain formless.

In order to understand how a temple becomes a place in which deity and humankind meet, it is necessary to grasp the symbolic meaning not only of the Hindu *mandira* but also of pilgrimage centers (*tirtha sthana*). The sacred images or icons (*murti*) also symbolize different aspects of the divine including creation, destruction, power, prosperity, strength, or protection. There is also a rich symbolism in the rituals, prayers, and artifacts used by the worshipper (*pujari*) during worship (*puja*).

THE HINDU *MANDIRA*

From the early Vedic period Hindus have tried to create a sacred space to which gods could descend and accept gifts from their followers. It would also provide a place in which people felt they could be with the gods and feel a sense of the Divine. During the later Vedic period prayers were conveyed to the gods through sacrificial fires believed to be manifestations of Agni, the god of fire. Through fires Vedic priests spiritually "ascended" to heaven. All such rites and ceremonies were performed in a sacred enclosure specifically prepared for communion with the gods. The tradition of this symbolic meeting of the human and the divine continues today in the Hindu *mandira*.

PREPARING THE GROUND

When a site has been selected for a temple, Hindus must ritually drive local spirits of the land away before construction begins. Then the ground is plowed and several seeds are sown. By observing the quality of the newborn plants the builder determines the quality of the soil. Next the earth is smoothed until it is perfectly flat, like a mirror. On this prepared land a circle is drawn, symbolizing heaven, and a square

WHERE THE GODS DWELL

A *mandira*, or Hindu temple, is constructed according to specific requirements. The site for a *mandira* is carefully selected. Brahmanic texts called Shilpa Shastras, written to direct architects and artisans, describe the requirements for such a site. One *purana* adds to the ideas about how to build a temple in a verse about its location. It says that "the gods always play where groves are near rivers, mountains, and springs and in towns with pleasure gardens . . . It is such places that the gods love and always dwell in."

SACRED MOUNTAINS

Motifs of mountains and caves are often incorporated skillfully into the architecture of the Hindu *mandira,* or temple. Throughout Hindu mythology mountains have been depicted as sacred. Mount Kailasha in the Himalayas is the abode of Shiva; Mount Meru, like a Hindu *mandira,* is believed to be the axis of the universe, joining celestial, atmospheric, and terrestrial regions. In fact the superstructure of a Hindu temple is called *shikhara,* meaning "the top of a mountain." Caves are also important natural symbols in Hinduism because as dark chambers with one small opening, they are believed to be symbolic of, and imbued with, the spirituality of the maternal womb. These chambers have traditionally served as ascetic retreats.

Mountain peaks in the Bhagirathi Valley in the Himalayas. The Bhagirathi River is one of the feeder streams for the sacred river Ganges whose source is in the Himalayas.

is drawn around the circle, symbolizing earth. It is believed that the center of this circle forms a sacred pillar connecting the "body" of the *mandira* with heaven. A small chest holding jewels and seeds and representing the essence of the temple is buried in the ground near the pillar. Above this the innermost sanctuary, the *garbhagrha,* or "womb chamber," is constructed.

EARLY HINDU TEMPLES

The earliest examples of Hindu temples were constructed around the fifth century C.E. These early stone temples were simple columned halls covered with a flat roof. Later this form developed into a square-columned hall raised on a flat, broad *bhumi,* or base (literally translated as "earth"), which led to the superstructure, a tower. The tower, or *shikhara* ("mountain peak"), was one of the most important parts of the *mandira.*

The *shikhara* rose at the rear of the *mandira.* It marked the location of the interior *garbhagrha* where the deity was believed to be enshrined. Divine light was believed to emit from this small, dark chamber and bless, protect, and watch over the community. Around this innermost shrine was a passageway on which devotees, moving clockwise, could encircle the inner chamber. The *garbhagrha* had just one opening, and only the presiding priest was allowed inside.

An assembly hall, the *mandapa,* was located in the sanctuary. This hall often led to another hall, the *natya mandapa,* where dances were performed and hymns sung to please the deities. These halls opened onto a veranda, which led to the outside.

The outer surface of the temple held detailed sculptures. Mythological scenes were depicted, juxtaposed with scenes from everyday life or important political events such as a royal coronation, conquests and celebrations, or portraits of royal and secular patrons. The main gateway leading toward the inner sanctuary of the temple was the only opening between sacred and profane spaces. Other openings—doors, niches, and windows—were architectural symbols of the passage of humanity to God.

Carved in Stone

By the eighth century many freestanding Hindu temples were carved from gigantic solid stone hills. One of these was the Shiva temple at Ellora (in the state of Maharashtra). Other sacred temples with detailed mythological scenes were carved in and around immense caves, such as Elephanta (in Maharashtra). These elaborate temple complexes were sculptural and architectural marvels.

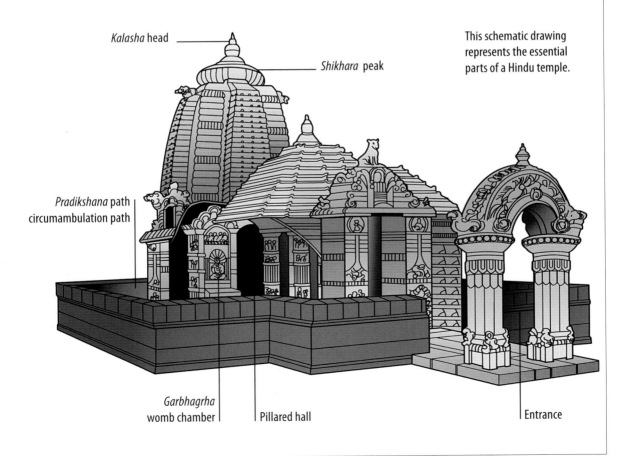

Kalasha head

Shikhara peak

This schematic drawing represents the essential parts of a Hindu temple.

Pradikshana path
circumambulation path

Garbhagrha
womb chamber

Pillared hall

Entrance

DIVINE KINGS AND KINGDOMS

Many temple complexes resembled the architecture used for palaces. This is not surprising given that deities were considered kings. The earthly kings, who were *mandira* patrons, were considered to be divine reflections of the deities. Their task was to watch over the welfare of their kingdoms. In some texts kings were described as supports or receptacles of gods. Sometimes kings were believed to be intermediaries between earth and heaven. It was their job to bring offerings of their subjects to the celestial region, and return with blessings from the gods. At times kings were believed to be incarnations of deities, meaning that they were the god in human form. If a king was particularly cruel or harsh, they were sometimes seen as incarnations of demons. The royal throne was often equated with the altar, and the temple was perceived as a divine fortress. The deity lived there and protected the world from chaos and disorder.

DEVOTIONS, GIFTS, AND GOOD KARMA

The *mandira* has always been a center for all artistic, intellectual, and religious life of the Hindu community. Dance, music, drama, art, and architecture were integral parts of the *mandira* rituals. Sacred dances and dramas were performed in the assembly halls.

Hindus praying before the innermost shrine, the *garbhagrha. Puja* offerings are given by worshippers to the priest, who performs *puja* on their behalf. Visitors also pray before the various smaller shrines in the temple and many will walk around the passageway surrounding the innermost shrine of the temple.

Mythological stories, recited earlier by storytellers and teachers were enacted in the *mandira*. Worshippers sang devotional songs and recited hymns from important scriptures, such as the Vedas, the *puranas,* and the epics.

During celebrations and festivals, the kings and rich citizens donated money, land, and valuable objects to the *mandira.* Some kings in southern India celebrated battle victories or the addition of a territory to their kingdom by bestowing magnificent gifts on the *mandira.* Inscriptions on the walls of these temples describe priceless necklaces of pearls and bright coral beads, as well as gold ornaments set in precious stones. These were donated to decorate the sacred images in the temples. Utensils of pure gold were given for daily services to the deities, and images of the most popular divinities—Nataraja, Vishnu, Rama, Krishna, Shiva, and Parvati—were presented to the temple.

Temple building and the installation of sacred images was not only an expression of devotion and piety but also a merit-gaining act, or an act of good karma. All donor devotees were promised peace, wealth, rich harvest, and sons if they erected a temple or donated an icon. In addition the generous gifts demonstrated physical importance and economic power to subjects and neighboring rulers.

EARTHLY DWELLINGS OF THE DEITIES

Today the Hindu *mandira* is considered a holy place in the midst of an irreligious world. As they always have been, temples and shrines are considered earthly dwelling places of the deities and a "crossing" where devotees of any caste can be with the divine. In a temple, worshippers believe that they can leave the illogical, earthly world behind and approach the eternal realm of knowledge and truth.

All Hindu communities have one or more local temples. Some are monumental, some are of average size, and some are quite small. Large temples are always devoted to one of the manifestations of the major deities like Shiva, Vishnu, or some form of Devi (Mahadevi Shakti). The smaller temples are devoted to minor regional deities known only to the local people. Hindus believe that they are linked with the sacred through these large temples and small shrines.

TIRTHA

Like Hindu temples, *tirtha sthana* (pilgrimage centers) are crossing places of the earthly and the spiritual worlds. *Tirtha* literally means a "crossing place" or a "ford," and in a *tirtha* worshippers feel closer to or even united with the deities. Journeying to a *tirtha* became popular because it was considered as beneficial to the pilgrim as Vedic sacrifices were to a Brahmin. Moreover, *tirtha* participation was accessible to devotees of all castes.

SACRED HISTORY AND SPIRITUAL MERIT

In these pilgrimage centers worshippers have access to the mythical personages, gods, goddesses, and saints who were either born

Temples lining Lake Pushkar in the state of Rajasthan. The town of Pushkar is particularly associated with the god Brahma.

or incarnated and who performed feats of austerity such as fasting and meditating for extremely long periods at these particular sites. People travel to far-off centers because they believe that the holy places radiate sacredness for the benefit of devotees. At the holy sites devotees feel closer to the sacred events that took place there and feel as though they were participating in the sacred history.

Most *tirtha sthana* are located in places that are difficult to reach. They are on the tops of mountains, deep in forests, or in the middle of deserts. Most are not accessible by modern transportation. To reach the holy destination pilgrims need self-discipline, endurance, and devotion. A pilgrim's effort is comparable to the austerities of an ascetic who has renounced worldly attachments and lives a life of fasting, meditation, and prayer. Hindus believe that they gain spiritual merit from the act. In addition a person may gain status in his community after having returned from a pilgrimage.

AN ENDLESS CYCLE OF LIVES

Hindus compare their time from birth to death to a pilgrim's journey with many stations. They do not consider death a final destination but just one station in an endless cycle of lives. Nor do Hindus believe that death automatically brings liberation from the frustrations of life. Rather they believe that *moksha* (final release) can be attained by complete devotion to God, knowledge of God, and through good works. Those who cannot liberate their atman (individual soul) through any of these means might attain it by completing a pilgrimage.

Pilgrimage brings spiritual joy and ultimate release from the world. By visiting a *tirtha sthana*, a devotee not only re-creates and participates in sacred history by being at the site of some mytho-

The word *murti* is used in the Upanishads and the Bhagavad Gita, and it implies much more than just a simple statue. Hindu icons visually express a strong sense of fantastic divine reality. For example the four arms of Vishnu, Ganesha's elephant head, or Skanda's six heads are all fantastic forms depicting a range of specific realities. As sacred statues these forms are easier for humankind to understand.

logical incident—but he or she is also able to visit the temples of these places that are charged with intense sacredness.

HINDU ICONS

In the Sanskrit language, a sacred statue is called *murti*. The term, which is more than 2,000 years old, refers to any figure that has a definite shape. Hindu icons, or sacred images, may be anthropomorphic—having human likeness—or they may be abstract. From the terra-cotta figurines of the Indus Valley to the modern images of Vishnu, *murtis* are considered genuinely sacred.

CHARGED WITH THE PRESENCE OF GOD

When icons are seen as personal deities, as in bhakti worship, they are considered to be charged with the presence of the god. Worshipping an image is one of the ways in which a devotee can gain access to a deity. The god is invited, bathed, adorned, touched, seen, and honored in the form of the *murti*, or sacred image. Therefore deep respect for the image of a goddess or god allows people to show their deep love for that goddess or god. Through the image devotees can pour out their emotions to the deity.

In addition to the size, shape, and artistic quality of a *murti*, there are many rituals that govern its actual making. First, it is important for the *shilpin*, or sculptor, to follow the advice of a Brahmin and gather the material for it following certain traditions. This means they would have to cut the tree or quarry the stone, depending on if the icon is made of wood or stone, at the proper time and in the proper manner. Because Hindus believe that each and every grain of matter is inhabited by local spirits, part of the ritual includes asking the spirits of the tree or rock to leave and dwell elsewhere. It is important to have a "clean" block of raw material, free of all spirits, on which to carve a divine image.

MEDITATION AND PURIFICATION

To make the icon, the *shilpins* first read about the image in the Shilpa Shastras. Then they focus mentally until they can form an image of the icon. Before starting the work a ritual purification must be performed. For a traditional image maker, creating an icon is equivalent to yogic discipline in that it requires intense meditation.

When an image is completed special rites of blessing take place. The image is purified with a variety of ritual substances such as clarified butter, honey, and a special kind of grass. In particular the eyes of the deity are sealed with the honey and butter. Then a priest installs various deities in different parts of the body of the icon by touching its individual parts. With this ritual a particular icon may be symbolically inhabited by a number of gods other than that which it depicts. Having many gods in one recalls the one body of the Vedic Primal Man (Purusha) and the deities created from it in the Vedic hymn *Purusha Shukta*.

Finally, breath is infused into the image through a rite called *pratishtha,* meaning "establishing the breathlike." During this rite a special mantra (secret verse) is uttered. Then the eyes are opened with a golden needle. After the blessing the icon is considered suitable for the deity to descend into it. Most of the images are established in this manner to invoke the presence of a deity. Without the complex rituals of purification and the rites of establishment, icons are plain works of art with no sacred power.

Icons of a deity rarely show the god in one form. Rather gods and goddesses are shown in their numerous manifestations. For instance Shiva is depicted as Nataraja or with Parvati. Vishnu is

---

CREATING A SACRED IMAGE

The Shilpa Shastras are texts that give detailed descriptions of how a sacred image ought to be created and made suitable for the presence of a deity. The texts provide measurements of body parts, the correct posture, number of hands and heads, hand gestures (*mudras*), emblems and weapons to be held, the appropriate *vahana* (animal vehicles), suitable sitting positions (*asana*), and more. An image must be proportionate, technically correct, and pleasing to the eye. Only then do Hindus believe that it will be fit for a deity's residence. Such specific details of the gods are the result of meditation, experimentation, and extreme devotion by generations of priests and artists.

shown in his various incarnations—Krishna, Rama, and others. Durga is sculpted as slaying her enemies in terrifying postures.

PUJA

Daily worship, or *puja,* is an important ritual in the lives of practicing Hindus. The daily rituals performed in the *mandira* are thought to be a source of prosperity and good health for the worshipper. The goal of *puja* is reminiscent of the Vedic fire sacrifice, in which gods were invited from the heavens and presented with offerings. *Puja* is the most frequently performed Hindu ritual.

CARING FOR THE DEITIES

Vedic people believed that deities lived in the heavens. By the epic period it was believed that divine power came to earth if a sacred area was made ritually pure, icons were consecrated, and the deity was persuaded with verbal chants to descend. Then the god or goddess was given constant love and honor. This was because the early Hindus believed that if proper devotion and care were given to the invited deity it would stay in the temple and watch over the community. If proper care of the images was not taken, and if the icons were not protected from vandalism and abuse, the deity would abandon it and the temple.

The idea of constant attention to a deity made it necessary for a daily routine of rituals. This resulted in the development of the Hindu *puja.* In each *mandira* a resident priest makes sure that at sunrise, noon, sunset, and midnight the proper *puja* is performed. In addition the priest resides in the temple so that continuous care may be taken and the god will always be present.

Visiting a *mandira* every day or even regularly is not mandatory for Hindus. Many devout Hindus keep in touch with their deities through worship at home. However, some rituals cannot be performed at home, and a priest's assistance is needed.

PUJA IN THE HOME

Puja is not congregational worship but an individual offering to a deity or to a deity and his or her companion. Reasons for

SEEING THE DEITIES

A *mandira,* or Hindu temple, has movable and immovable sacred images called *murtis.* Immovable images are part of the temple architecture, whereas movable images can be taken out during festival days to allow devotees to "see" the deities. *Darsana,* or seeing images of deities, becomes a significant act whether the deity is at home, at the temple, or journeying in a procession. This rite of seeing is one of the basic components of Hindu worship.

The center of attention during various celebrations is the image of Ganesha, the elephant-headed son of Shiva. The deity is carried on a ceremonial chariot and paraded through the streets for everyone to see.

Puja—daily worship—consists of three ritual steps: first, seeing the deity (*darsana*); second, *puja*, or worship, which includes offering flowers, fruits, and cooked food called *bhog*; and third, retrieving the blessed food, called *prasada*, and consuming it. By these sacred acts Hindus create a relationship with the divinity through their emotions and senses. As one scholar writes, "The temple is the monument of [divine] manifestations. The devotee who comes to the temple to look at it, does so as a seer, not as a mere spectator."

temple worship could be related to personal or family health, wealth, education, general blessings, or safety. Many strive for good karma or liberation (*mukti*). Present-day rituals of *puja*, at home and in the temple, have not altered much from what was practiced during the earliest periods, although the ancient rituals have been greatly simplified.

In their homes most Hindus keep a shrine dedicated to one or more deities. The shrine contains images of the family deity, major gods and goddesses, saints, and ancestors. It is kept in a sacred area, which may be a corner of a room, a niche, a shelf of a cabinet or, in an affluent household, a small room set aside solely for this purpose. Other ritual paraphernalia include a container of water for sprinkling and purifying the area, a bell, a lamp to be waved in front of the deity, an incense burner, and a tray with flowers, fruit, and freshly cooked food. At the household shrine all members of a Hindu family offer a simple daily *puja*.

PUJA IN THE MANDIRA

In the home the deities are invited to descend. In the *mandira*, on the other hand, they are "awakened," because the temple their earthly home. The gods are believed to dwell in the *mandira* as royalty. At the *mandira* full *puja* is performed several times every day. It differs from the daily *puja* performed at a home more in scale than in substance. In the temples that enshrine major Brahmanic gods, priests who celebrate full *puja* are referred to as Brahmins. Smaller temples and shrines of minor deities may be presided over by a member of a lower caste.

The light within a *mandira* is dim, a sharp contrast to the bright light outside. The *mandapa* (assembly hall) is charged with the scent of flowers, burning oil lamps, and incense. A devotee walks slowly toward the innermost sanctuary of the deity with the ingredients for *puja*, which may include flowers, fruit, and cooked *bhog*. Near the sanctuary these things are handed to the priest, who then performs *puja* on behalf of the worshipper.

After seeing the image and receiving the *prasada*, or sacred food, the devotee walks around the passageway of the sanctuary. The ritual of *pradikshana*—encircling the womb chamber clockwise and touching the outer walls of the innermost sanctuary—is an important part of the *mandira* ritual that cannot be performed at home. Walking around an image, the inner sanctum, or the *mandira* itself is a way of paying respect to the deity, for movement is considered an important part of *puja*.

SEEING, TOUCHING, AND HEARING

In addition to prayers and offerings Hindu worship includes an understanding of the godly image, an experience charged with religious meaning. This experience is encouraged by the ancient act of "seeing." It is not only the worshipper "seeing" the image but also the deity "seeing" the worshipper that is considered a favorable act. This act is called *darsana*. For this reason Hindu images have strikingly large eyes to facilitate the "exchange of glances" between devotee and deity.

Similarly, in *puja* one does not only see but also touches and hears. All the senses are given special significance and importance in *puja*. One observes the offering of the lighted lamps, touches the ritual objects and feet of the deity (where possible), hears the ringing of the bells and the sacred texts being recited, smells the incense, and tastes the blessed food offered at the end of the ritual.

INVITING DEITIES TO DESCEND

During the *puja*, or daily worship, at a home shrine the head of a Hindu household invites the goddess or god to descend and be present at the ceremony. When the divine presence is felt, worshippers consider that the deity has entered the *murti*, or sacred image, and they offer it a seat, wash its feet, and give water to it. An image might be symbolically bathed, then clothed in new garments and embellished with ornaments. Perfumes and ointments are often applied; flowers and garlands are placed before it. Incense is burned and a burning lamp is waved in front of the deity. Foods such as cooked rice, fruit, butter, and sugar are offered. Family members bow before the image, sip the blessed water, and receive a portion of the cooked food, which, having been blessed by the deity, is now considered sacred food for the devotees. Finally the deity is asked to rest or depart.

THE WORSHIPPER

A Hindu worshipper, or *pujari,* may perform daily *puja* at home and on special days in the *mandira. Pujaris* must be physically healthy as well as ritually clean before starting to worship. They must take a bath, wear fresh clothes, and free their minds of any impure thoughts. A priest must also be physically and ritually clean. Through purifying acts priests and worshippers are able to identify themselves with the divine object of worship.

In worship devotees see divine images and mythological scenes on the outer walls of the *mandira.* These help the worshippers to recall all the sacred stories they have heard about or read. With their minds full of the stories and their senses full from worship, devotees believe that they come to know that which is unknowable. Through art, architectural forms, and devotion, the worshipper can find new spiritual meaning in things.

A Hindu boy praying before a family shrine in India. Most families keep a household shrine dedicated to one or more deities. During *puja,* the head of the household will invite the goddess or god to descend and be present throughout the *puja.*

The doorway of the *mandira* is believed to be vulnerable to the evils of the outside world. Therefore minor divinities such as door guardians and images of sacred rivers are carved on or placed near lintels and doorjambs. These images are thought to cleanse devotees of any mental or physical impurities. They also bestow divine blessings on them as they enter the *mandira*.

MOVING TOWARD THE DIVINE

Inside the *mandira* worshippers are said to move toward the divine. They walk through a series of enclosures that become increasingly more sacred. As a person passes through these enclosures he or she is gradually raised from an earthly level to a sacred level.

In the *mandira* the worshippers do not physically ascend to heaven but by focusing spiritually they may gain a divine enlightenment. From open spaces they reach closed spaces; from light they enter darkness; from the complexity of the world they move to the simplicity of the divine. In the final stage the worshippers approach the doorway of the *garbhagrha* ("womb chamber") and hand their offerings to the priest, who then conducts *puja* for them. They wait outside, following the movements of the priest.

SACRED RITES AND DIVINE LOVE

A common part of Hindu worship is the gestures of humility such as bowing, kneeling, lying prostrate, and the touching of feet. Honor and affection are expressed by doing for the god what one does daily for cherished family members. Family activities such as waking, bathing, dressing, cooking, serving, and sleeping become refined by daily practice. Hindu *puja* consists of doing these day-to-day activities to honor personal gods. Mundane daily acts, when refined, become ritual acts fit to be performed for the family deity. Finally, at the special time of *puja*, the god is invited, bathed, adorned, touched, seen, and honored. The secular feelings become charged with sacred intensity. Human feelings become divine love. Thus the family relationships and ritual acts of *puja* are closely interwoven. Routine chores become sacred rites when performed in honor of a deity.

CHAPTER 7

SOCIAL DUTY AND RITES OF PASSAGE

The term *dharma,* meaning "moral duty or law," is important in Hinduism. The origin and meaning of this word goes back as far as the Vedic period, when the word *rita* meant "cosmic order." According to the divine law of *rita,* all things in the world have a proper place, function, and order. This creates a balance in the universe.

In Vedic times, cosmic order included the duty to be moral. In the Shastra texts, the idea of *rita* branched into the diverse concepts of dharma. In those texts, *dharma* meant not only cosmic law and moral duty but also social, ethical, and religious duty. Shastras emphasize that the reality of the universe depends on the proper behavior of the people. An improper action, that is, *adharma,* can lead to the fall of the universe into unreality and eventually into nothingness. Therefore in order to maintain the universe and enhance cosmic harmony, proper behavior is necessary. Dharma, then, is responsible for the maintenance of the Hindu world.

Hindu marriage rites are performed in front of a fire pit made of bricks. The bride and groom, their immediate families and the priest encircle the fire for the wedding ritual and *puja.* At the end of the ceremony the bride and groom take seven steps around the fire.

In Hinduism the moral and social duties of dharma are tied to the theories of karma, samsara, and ultimately, *moksha*. Therefore it is important to learn about these three terms before discussing Hindu *varnasramadharma*, a system of duty or law that includes the four castes and the four stages of life.

ORIGINS OF DHARMA

The ideas of ethical behavior and moral life come from sacred Hindu literature. Traditionally Hindu literature has been divided into two classes. One class is *shruti* ("what is heard"), covering the Vedas and Upanishads. The other is *smriti* ("what is remembered"), covering the epics and the *puranas*. The *smriti* literature also includes a literary form called sutras.

The sutras were written by the Brahmins before the beginning of the present era. It perhaps seemed to the later Vedic Brahmins that one's religious life should be concerned with more than rituals—their texts describe how leading an ethical life is an integral part of religious life. The Brahmins do not deny that the rituals are sacred, but they stress the importance of ethical behavior, give instructions in social duty, and teach sacred morality. Their texts were called Dharma Sutras.

The Dharma Sutras were difficult to understand. Therefore these texts were explained and expanded into compositions called Dharma Shastras. The shastras were written in verse and they were easier to memorize and grasp than the Dharma Sutras. Eventually Hindus turned to the Dharma Shastras as guides to ideal social behavior. The shastras say that those who support dharma gain fame while alive and incomparable happiness after death. To support dharma is to behave in an ethical manner. The term *dharma* therefore is closely related to the idea of karma—that one's actions in the present determine the conditions of one's life in the future.

Sutra

The sutras provided moral teachings. The word *sutra* literally means "a thread," and its content was to be memorized in addition to the Vedas. The earliest of the sutras were the Griha Sutras (domestic rituals) and Surata Sutras (priestly rituals). The last of the series were compositions called Dharma Sutras (ways of moral behavior).

KARMA AND SAMSARA

Originally any correct activity or properly performed ritual was called karma. However, later religious philosophers expanded its meaning. It came to mean that one's present actions determine one's future life. Thus underlying the Hindu law of karma is the idea that a person's behavior leads to an appropriate reward or punishment.

Some scholars think that the idea that a future life depended on previous behavior must have developed from a long period of keenly observing plants, trees, and fields. These scholars believe that the early Hindus noted that land "gives birth" repeatedly if healthy seeds are sown and tended. They saw that plants do not really die; the death of a plant is a process by which it renews itself in the spring. In a sense each life of a plant ends in a death in order to be reborn. A plant's regrowth is determined by the healthy or unhealthy conditions of former births. Scholars believe the early Hindus felt the same to be true of all living things.

During the Vedic period proper ritual performance was called karma. In that era if a priest performed certain rituals correctly he was believed to control the gods. Later Upanishadic seers taught our current understanding of karma. They believed that all physical and mental activity was a reflection of greater cosmic processes. They taught that a person becomes good through good actions and bad through bad actions. Through these seers the concept of the cycles of life, death, rebirth, and redeath was reinforced. These cycles were called samsara.

The theories of karma and samsara provide Hindus with a reason for human differences. If people are of differing social classes or physical and mental abilities it

> ### Laws of Manu
>
> The most influential of all the Dharma Shastras was written by a sage named Manu. This text, written some time between 200 B.C.E. and 200 C.E., is known as the Laws of Manu. The *Laws of Manu* seems to have established the public norm of today's Hindu society.

Sadhus bathing at the Maha Kumbha Mela, the great religious fair and mass ritual bathing that takes place every 12 years at Allahabad. Ritual bathing in sacred rivers, particularly at the Kumbha Mela, is a spiritual act that cleanses the body and mind and improves karma.

must be a result of their deeds in this life or a past life. Karma and samsara also encourage Hindus to act ethically, because if they do not they will suffer for their poor actions in the future.

The samsara cycles are an ever-changing universe of requirements, consequences, and conditions. This universe contrasts with the unconditioned and eternal world of the gods. The goal of practicing Hindus is to liberate themselves from constantly changing samsara—to find release from the cycles of rebirths and redeaths and gain existence in the realm of the gods.

MOKSHA

Moksha is the release from the conditional and temporary existence of this world. It is a religious state for which every Hindu strives. *Moksha* cannot be gained by action aimed at achieving something in this world. Rather the person who wants liberation from life—*mukti*—seeks to experience the oneness of atman-Brahman, the union of one's self with the Ultimate Reality.

Moksha is not a Vedic concept. The Vedic texts are concerned with enjoyment of earthly bounties. Vedic people were awed by natural powers. They composed and chanted hymns to appease the personifications of natural forces and invite these personified gods to share the bounties of the earth. Vedic people did not want release from the good earthly life.

In Indian thought the notion of *moksha* appeared as early as the oldest Upanishad, and the concept is elaborated on in the epic Mahabharata and the Dharma Shastras.

A Hindu is supposed to model his life according to the dharmic norm prescribed in the *Laws of Manu*. He or she must obey caste laws and follow the stages of life. If the person leads an ideal life as described in the sacred text, he or she may then learn detachment from material life and achieve liberation. This ideal Hindu life is reflected in the model of *varnasramadharma*.

VARNASRAMADHARMA

Varnasramadharma is a term that combines three separate words: *varna*, meaning the social caste system; *ashrama*, meaning the stages of life; and *dharma*, which means duty, law, or proper behavior. *Varnsramadharma* is based on reciprocal social obligations. It was described in Dharma Shastras as a guide for male members of the Hindu community. Later it became a system for Hindu society in general. *Varnasramadharma* and samsara give moral, ethical, and social values to members of the Hindu community and form the basis of the Hindu society.

Varnasramadharma is a guide to living with the laws of dharma and karma. Within this system Hindus support one another by performing the duties of their particular *varna*. Hindus believe that if one person does his or her duty imperfectly it harms the entire society and thus the universe as a whole. One person's dharma, or duty, cannot be performed by another. As the Bhagavad Gita says, "It is better to perform one's own obligations poorly than to do another's well."

These ideals of the four castes and the four stages of life were set forth in the Hindu texts. However in practice not many men went beyond the stage of householder. However, the possibility was open for a householder to pursue the life of a forest dweller in order to achieve *moksha*.

VARNA

The *Laws of Manu* affirm that the Vedic hymn *Purusha Shukta* is the Hindu justification for its social system—*varna*. The

CASTE AND THE STAGES OF LIFE

The system of *varnasramadharma*, guidance on social responsibilities through the various stages of life, was stimulated by the coming of outsiders. It was created to keep foreigners away from the core of society. It also served to organize the diverse occupations of Hindus and make a householder's position strong. This model evolved by combining two social ideals. The first is that of *varna*, the four hierarchical castes (Brahmins, Kshatriyas, Vaishyas, and Shudras). The second is that of *ashrama*, or the male member's four stages of life—*brahmachari* (student), *grahasthin* (householder), *vanaprasthin* (forest dweller), and *sanyasin* (ascetic).

Sanatana Dharma

As a general rule all the important Hindu texts assert that people, regardless of their age and occupation, should observe some common moral obligations. For example, everyone must tell the truth, practice goodwill, be forgiving, and exercise patience at all times. Such rules, in addition to *varnasramadharma*, are called *sanatana* (eternal) or *sadharana* (pertaining to everyone). Hindus commonly call their religion *Sanatana Dharma*.

hymn refers to social divisions believed to be typical of the Aryans who immigrated to the Indus Valley and the Ganges plains. These were the Vedic people. There is no historical record that defines *varna*, but it appears from the Vedic hymns that the social system was composed of four major subdivisions—the Brahmins, the priestly class; Kshatriyas, nobles or warriors; Vaishyas, the merchants and farmers; and Shudras, the servant class.

An important condition of the four social orders, taught in the Bhagavad Gita, was that they were not rigidly defined by a person's birth. They were to be judged according to a person's nature rather than the family into which they were born. However, this spiritual teaching was rarely applied as the system became rigid and complex. As time went on the caste system became inflexible. A person's duty varied according to his caste and to the stage of life he or she was passing through. Moreover an individual's sex, family, and region further complicated the matter.

CASTE AND SUBCASTE

At present the *varna* system has developed into *jatis* (subcastes) because of intercaste and interracial marriages. When members of the same caste married, the same caste continued for the next generation. When members of different castes married, their offspring generated a new caste. This new generation belonged to a caste lower than the three upper castes but higher than Shudra (the lowest). However, if a member of any of the three upper classes married a Shudra or a member of any other race, their children were "untouchables." These children belonged to a class lower than the Shudras. This complicated system resulted in the creation of thousands of *jatis*.

Hindus belonging to these *jatis* live throughout India. They have rules governing marriage, food, occupation, and other

---

Purusha Shukta

The idea that the world is balanced when it is made up of distinct social classes, or castes, is rooted in this Vedic hymn called *Purusha Shukta*.

When they divided the Man (Purusha) into how many parts did they divide him. What was his mouth, what were his arms, What were his thighs and his feet called?

The Brahmin was his mouth, of his arms was made Kshatriya, his thighs became the Vaishya, of his feet the Shudra was born.

activities. This is done to keep family purity. Punishment for disobeying the rules of marriage results in expulsion from the *jati* to which one belongs.

For many Hindus the *jatis* are simply subdivisions of the classical *varna*. Belonging to a particular *varna* through their *jati* is important because they believe that it plays a part in the reward or punishment each soul receives for its actions during a previous existence. For Hindus present life conditions have something to do with the purity and sanctity of Brahmins and the high or low rank attributed to each *jati*. However, social caste is believed to be due mainly to the life led by a soul in its previous incarnations. Brahmins are supposed to have the purest souls. If a Brahmin is wicked, however, he may be reborn as a member of a much lower caste or even as an untouchable as punishment.

THE FOUR *VARNAS*

The four *varnas* make up a workable system that depicts all members of society supporting one another. Brahmins, at the top of the system, were formerly required to teach the Vedas, assist in sacrifices, and accept gifts. No other caste under any circumstances could perform these three duties. The top priority of the Brahmins was maintaining the purity of their class for the purpose of domestic and temple rituals. Vegetarianism was encouraged and eventually became a norm among Brahmins. Thus Brahmins who "were not desirous of killing" retained their higher rank in society.

Kshatriyas were rulers and warriors. As kings they had power on earth. They protected their subjects and looked after the proper functioning of the society. As warriors their caste duty was to slay enemies. They could study but not teach the Vedas.

Vaishyas on the other hand had the duty of breeding cattle. In addition they were agriculturists and moneylenders. They could study the Vedas, offer sacrifices, and offer sacred gifts. Moreover they too participated in the rites of passage and wore the sacred thread. However, the Vaishyas were not permitted to perform religious rites or the duties of a warrior.

Shudras performed only minor sacrifices and simplified domestic rituals that did not require reciting from the Vedas. They did all sorts of manual work so that society as a whole could function smoothly. They were not permitted to perform any sacred rituals. Furthermore they were not officially initiated into the system of *varnasramadharma*, although they took care of the basic necessities of the society.

BRAHMACHARI, THE STUDENT

As a student, or *brahmachari*, a Hindu male was to study diligently in order to know the sacred traditions and literature. Between the ages of eight and 12 a boy of any of the three upper castes could study the Vedas after he was initiated by a teacher who had accepted him as a student. The boy went through a rite of initiation before he was allowed to live with his teacher. Once accepted he was instructed in the recitation of the sacred texts.

In the teacher's ashram the student lived a life of poverty and submission. He was supposed to live as a personal servant of the teacher and do all of his teacher's daily chores, such as toting fuel and water, serving food, and cleaning up. He was expected to show great devotion and respect to his teacher. He completed his studies after several years of living in this austere manner.

Ashramas

Ashramas are viewed as the four rungs in the ladder leading up to liberation, or *moksha*. Although the student stage is the time for preparation for adult life, the householder stage is the most important stage in this system. The forest dweller and ascetic stages are regarded as belonging to the time of old age and retirement. Persons situated in each *ashrama* are expected to pay respect to those who belong to a higher stage than they do.

GRAHASTHIN, THE HOUSEHOLDER

When the young man completed his studies he was expected to marry. This was considered the second *ashrama*, that of *grahasthin*, the householder. The man was expected to earn a living for himself, beget sons, and take care of his family by doing work appropriate to his caste. In addition as a householder he was expected to give alms to those who had passed into the higher *ashrama*, that of the forest dweller and ascetic.

Marriage and begetting sons were immensely important in this *ashrama*. The relationship between husband and wife is described in the Dharma Shastras. As long as the wife lived she was not to do anything to displease her husband. After his death she was to remain devoted to his memory and was never to even utter the name of another man.

VANAPRASTHIN, THE FOREST DWELLER

When a man had fulfilled his duties as the head of the family, when his skin was wrinkled and his hair white, he was expected to retire from family life and proceed with his wife toward the higher *ashrama—vanaprasthin—*that of the forest dweller. The forest dweller contributed to the welfare of the society by performing rituals in honor of his ancestors. However, only a very small percentage of people really left home in order to live in the forest away from family and community. Most people paid homage to their ancestors while living at home and went on pilgrimages each year to be closer to the gods.

SANYASIN, THE ASCETIC

The last *ashrama* in one's life, *sanyasin,* became necessary if one wished to achieve liberation. The difference between a forest dweller and an ascetic was that the ascetic renounced all connection with wife and family. Perhaps seclusion from family and community for a period of time—that is, living the life of a forest dweller—was essential before one could completely give up the world physically as well as mentally.

It was only at this fourth stage that one could understand the mystery of the divine, experience its presence, and possibly have communion with it. A forest dweller who was not a *sanyasin* could keep in touch with the world in general, but the ascetic stayed completely away from it. Living his life with only the most basic personal items, he had no physical comfort. His whole day was devoted to meditation, reflection, and the reading of Upanishadic scriptures. It was believed that this simple yet serene state of the *sanyasin* continued beyond death and that such people never returned to this world. Such ascetics are esteemed in Hindu society and are entitled to special respect and support.

Ashramas and *varnas* form two pillars of the Hindu social and family systems of the *Sanatana Dharma*. Besides teaching the significance of the caste system and four stages of life, the sacred texts of the Brahmanic tradition also describe some rituals that should be performed at strategic points in a Hindu's life.

CELEBRATIONS AND RITES OF PASSAGE

The Hindu calendar is a lunar one, with eleven months, and a twelfth one added every three or four years to bring the calendar back into line with the solar calendar. Major festivals occur in each season.

Rituals performed and celebrated at the time of important transitions in the life of a Hindu, from the moment of conception to the time of death, are called *samskaras*. There are four major

Colored pink and red by powder that has been thrown in celebration at the festival of Holi, a procession makes its way along a pilgrimage path in the town of Vrindavan, northern India.

rites of passage, passed down in the mainstream Brahmanic tradition and described in the shastras. These are the prenatal, childhood, marriage, and death rituals.

On such occasions family members and friends join together to bless the individual and to protect him or her from any harm. All major rituals are performed at home. Family priests are called in to perform the most important rituals, but family members are usually the primary performers of the home rituals.

PRENATAL RITUALS

Three rites are performed before the birth of a child: the rite of conception, the wish for a male child, and protection of the fetus. To ensure the fertility and safety of the mother and child, the rite of conception is performed long before there is any news of the arrival of a child. In the third or fourth month of pregnancy a rite is performed to ensure the birth of a male child. This ceremony also contains rites and safeguards against miscarriages. Finally, between the fourth and the eighth month of pregnancy, a rite is performed to protect the fetus from evil spirits.

CHILDHOOD RITUALS

A number of rituals are performed between a child's birth and adolescence. The first is a simple ritual performed immediately after birth. The most important is the second ritual, known as the naming ceremony, which is held on the 10th or 12th day after the birth of the baby. On this occasion the baby is given a formal name. The third ritual is celebrated when a baby is weaned from its mother and given solid food to eat for the first time. This is celebrated sometime in the sixth month. Between the ages of one and five girls experience a ceremonial ear piercing and boys have their first haircut. These two traditional ceremonies conclude the childhood rites.

UPANAYANA—THE SACRED THREAD

Many of the childhood and adolescence rituals are aimed at protecting and nurturing the child. However, others have social sig-

MONTHS OF THE HINDU LUNAR CALENDAR AND MAJOR FESTIVALS

Chaitra   March/April
Rama Naumi – The birthday of Rama, the hero of the Ramayana and the seventh incarnation of the god Vishnu.

Vaishakha   April/May

Jyaishtha   May/June

Ashadha   June/July
Ratha Yatra – Originating the town of Puri, an image of Vishnu is placed on a huge wooden chariot and pulled through the streets.

Shravana   July/August
Raksha Bandhan – A thread made of silk and decorated with flowers is tied by sisters around the wrists of their brothers to signify affection and protection.

Bhadra   August/September
Janmashtami – The birthday of Krishna, teacher of the Bhagavad Gita and the eighth incarnation of the god Vishnu.

Ashvina   September/ October
Navaratri or Durga Puja – Devi, the female form of the divine power, is worshipped in various forms. The festival lasts for nine nights. On the 10th day the festival of Dussehra is celebrated, when Durga's victory over a demon is recalled as well as Rama's victory over Ravana.
Divali – The five-night festival of lights honoring Lakshmi, the goddess of prosperity. It is also a celebration of the triumphant return of Rama and Sita to their kingdom.

Kartika   October/November

Agrahyana   November/December

Pausa   November/December

Magha   January/February
Mahashivaratri – "The great night of Shiva" when Hindus offer special worship to Shiva, his consort Parvati, and their son Ganesha.
Sarasvati – The first day of the spring season, when the goddess Sarasvati, patron of the arts and learning, is honored.

Phalguna   February/March
Holi – A celebration of the grain harvest; also a time when Krishna's pranks are recalled with the boisterous throwing of colored water and powder.

In each month Shukla Paksha is the two-week period of the waxing moon and Krishna Paksha is the two-week period of the waning moon.

nificance. Through them the young child is prepared to assume the social and religious responsibilities of the adult world.

The main ritual of adolescence is the Vedic initiation rite called *upanayana* (popularly known as the thread ceremony). It is regarded as the second birth of the initiate. Only male children of the three upper castes (Brahmins, Kshatriyas, and Vaishyas) go through this ceremony of initiation into their respective classes.

Males who take part in the *upanayana* ritual are called twice born because they are spiritually reborn at this ceremony. Their first birth, from their mother's womb, is considered incomplete. At the *upanayana* ceremony the children are "born again" as members of the Hindu social system. Members of the fourth caste, Shudras, traditionally did not go through this ceremony. However it is now generally accepted that a member of the Shudra caste who aspires to the spiritual path can be "born again" through initiation and take up sacred work. Before the ritual of initiation

A baby's hair is being shaved for the first time. This is one of the Hindu *samskaras,* rituals performed to mark the important stages in the life of a Hindu. This ritual haircutting happens when the child is one, three, or five years old.

the children of higher classes are considered the same as Shudras. Men of the three higher castes who remain uninitiated after the ages of 16, 22, and 24, respectively, are regarded as impure, and social interaction with them is forbidden.

COMPLETING THE CEREMONY

Before the ritual of *upanayana* the boy eats his last meal with his mother. From that moment he is expected to eat with the adult male members of his family. His head is then shaved and he is bathed. He wears a girdle of deerskin (nowadays replaced by cotton material), carries a wooden staff, and is finally given the sacred thread.

After the completion of this ceremony the young man, along with the priest, puts wood into the sacred fire. This is the boy's first encounter with the sacrifice, the central religious act of the Vedic religion. Formerly the pupil remained for many years after the ceremony at the teacher's house, away from his own home and family. During this time he had no status, rank, or property. Rather he led a life of humility, obedience, and chastity. In present times many young men perform this ritual before they go to college, or even later, before they get married. Modern young men do not live with the teacher unless they have decided to devote their lives to the study of scriptures.

At the completion of his studies another ritual incorporates the student into Hindu society. In modern times this ritual takes place when a child graduates from college or university and returns to his parents' home. The central theme of this ritual is a ceremonial bath. After the bath the student becomes a full-fledged member of the community. He is ready to marry and become a householder and to take on all the commitments and responsibilities associated with that. The search for a suitable bride begins.

A Brahmin priest conducts the sacred thread ceremony with a Hindu boy. This thread, or *upavita*, consists of three cords, each of which is made by twisting three strands. The *upavita* is a visible symbol of all individual existences, inseparable and linked to one single source of the universe. The thread is normally worn over the left shoulder and hangs under the right arm. It is regarded as the central component of the initiation rituals.

MARRIAGE

Marriage (*vivah*) is one of the most important rituals in the life of a Hindu. Only a married man is allowed to perform principal religious sacrifices. In addition he is the only one who takes care of family members belonging to all four *ashramas* of life (unmarried men are responsible only for relatives who belong to the first two *ashramas*). Thus a married man's role is pivotal in Hindu society. However, such a man is considered complete only after begetting a son.

The first step in the *vivah* is finding a suitable match. The parents make their choice with the child's consent. Then, with the help of an astrological calendar and the family priest, they decide on a favorable day for the marriage ritual.

THE MARRIAGE RITES

The betrothal takes place sometime before the day of the marriage. On the wedding day the groom usually goes to the bride's house in a colorful procession along with many friends and relatives. The bride wears bright red attire, symbolizing love and faith, and the groom wears white traditional dress, symbolizing purity and serenity. The father of the groom asks for the bride's hand and the bride's father formally offers it. The marriage ritual is conducted by a family priest belonging to the Brahmin class. Although the main ritual varies from region to region, the four basic rites remain the same and form the core of the ceremony.

The rites are performed in front of a fire pit made of bricks. The priest sits close to the fire, Agni, with the bride, the groom, and the parents of the bride and groom. The invited family and friends encircle this group while the priest performs the wedding rites. In the wedding ritual, as in *puja*,

A Hindu bride and her female relatives celebrate her marriage in rural India.

bells are rung, the Vedic hymns are chanted, and fragrant flowers, clarified butter (butter that has been cooked to separate the milk solids and water from the butter fat), uncooked grain, and many other such ingredients are poured as oblations into Agni.

THE SEVEN STEPS

Amid the festive sounds, sweet smells, and vibrant colors the bridegroom says to the bride that he will take care of her health and happiness. He then guides her three times around the fire. After each complete turn he recites a mantra. He tells her, "Be my friend. May you be devoted to me. Let us have many sons. May they reach old age." Then the couple takes seven steps around the fire. The taking of the seven steps is the most important part of the ceremony. To symbolize their union the bride and the groom eat a common meal while sitting together. After the marriage ritual the couple goes to the husband's home, and on the fourth day several rites are performed to ensure fertility.

CREMATION AND THE LAST RITES

When someone dies family and friends are informed as quickly as possible. Within a few hours the dead body is carried on a litter in a procession to the local cremation ground. The procession is led by the eldest son, acting as the chief mourner of the deceased. The name of a god—either Rama, Hari (Krishna), or Shiva—is cried out as the procession moves. At the cremation ground the body is laid on a specially prepared pyre of wood and is cremated in the belief that its soul will be united with the ancestors after the proper funerary rit-

---

THE LAST SACRIFICE

Cremation has been the customary way of taking care of human remains since the earliest period of Indian history. Cremation was regarded as the last sacrifice, antyesti, in which one's own body is offered in the sacred fire, Agni. It is believed that from the fire the deceased person is born again into a new existence in the company of his or her ancestors.

A body being burned in a funeral pyre on the cremation ghats at Pashupatinath on the bank of the River Bagmati in Kathmandu, Nepal.

uals are performed. The mourners return to their homes without looking back.

The funerary ritual, *sraddha,* is performed in order to help the deceased reach the homes of the ancestors safely. It is believed that after the cremation the people who have died pass through a period when they live as ghosts. During this period, which may last as long as one year, they are dangerous and their relatives are impure. Offerings of food and water are made for the newly deceased in the ritual of *sraddha.* Balls of rice and libations of water are offered, accompanied by the recitation of texts expressing respect and concern. The death rituals are the rites of passage from the earthly existence to the world of the fathers. They last anywhere from 12 days to a year, depending on the beliefs of the person who is performing them.

The prenatal, childhood, marriage, and death rituals are also performed for women belonging to the twice-born castes (the castes that take part in the sacred thread ceremony). During these times Vedic formulas are not recited, since women are not allowed to read or hear the Vedas. Indeed, within the system of *varnasramadharma,* women were not believed to be spiritually inclined. They did not enter into any of the stages of life, they were dependent on their fathers as young girls, on their husbands as women, and in their old age they were the responsibility of their sons.

CHAPTER 8

INNOVATIONS AND MODERN HINDUISM

The religious life of Hindus today is usually centered around bhakti, *puja*, rituals and festivals performed at home and in the temple, and the *varnasramadharma* system of duties and obligations. Some Hindus follow all of these traditions and others just a few. Thousands of modern Hindus practice another ancient tradition—that of devotion to saints. The saints have led the innovative movements in Hinduism.

THE ROLE OF THE SAINTS

In Hinduism saints, meaning those individuals who have been activists for the religion, have been pivotal in generating and spreading new ideas rooted in ancient traditions. The extraordinary saint-poets of the epics and the *puranas* and the bhakti movement made Brahmanism available to the common people. During Islamic rule the wandering minstrels kept Hindu beliefs and traditions alive without changing Hinduism's internal structure. During the 19th century modern Hindus rediscovered their forgotten scriptures as they came face to face with the Industrial

Holi festival celebrations In Nandgaon, central India. Celebrating the grain harvest but also called the festival of colors, Holi is a popular Hindu spring festival dedicated to Krishna and his beloved Radha. Nandgaon is a religious place due to its attachment to Krishna, as it is believed he spent his childhood in the village.

Revolution and Christianity. This environment led to new religious movements.

Each century has given rise to hundreds of such saints. Some become popular only after death, others while still alive. Some of these are much esteemed, others go unnoticed. Some are wandering mystics leading a life of asceticism, others are quite practical. Some are illiterate, others have doctorates from universities. However, all of these saints have certain things in common: they are completely devoted to the divine, have love and compassion for humanity, and are sensitive toward the universe.

Today many living saints look after their followers' physical and mental well-being in rapidly changing times. Their popularity is not due to their strict adherence to the ancient scriptures. Rather it comes from their roles in bringing about relevant changes needed and desired by the common people.

THE HINDU DIASPORA

As a result of migration over the last 50 years or more, major Hindu communities now exist around the world, making Hinduism for the first time in its history a truly universal religion. However, as with all such faiths, the problems of maintaining the traditional beliefs and practices is proving difficult, and as a result many communities worry about how to ensure that their traditions are passed on. Summer schools, special lessons, and involvement in religious festivals are some of the ways these communities seek to ensure continuity.

INTERFAITH DIALOGUE

The interaction between Hindu communities in the diaspora and other faith communities has led to a considerable interest within Hinduism in interfaith dialogue. Hinduism is present at all such interfaith events. The move toward this dialogue

The Path of Yoga

Modern Hindu gurus, or teacher-saints, follow one of the many religious ways, of which the path of yoga is the most common. Through the exercises of mind and body, yoga teaches techniques for achieving self-insight and mental balance. These living saints teach their followers how to gain peace, shed superficial values, become loving and compassionate, and feel one with each other and with the universe.

looks back to the 1893 Chicago World's Fair and the role that Swami Vivekananda played in opening the idea of faiths working together. Leading Hindu intellectuals such as Dr. Karan Singh have carried this message further and deeper than even Swami Vivekananda could have imagined.

ENVIRONMENTAL AND ECONOMIC ACTION

Alongside the interfaith movement Hindus have also become active in the environmental movement. Across India and in other parts of the world Hindu communities are seeking ways to protect nature. In particular they are examining again their ancient tradition of sacred forests and sacred groves, which in the past offered sanctuary not just to human beings but to all of nature.

In other spheres Hindus are examining their economic role. The rise of faith-consistent investing has led to some commercial banking and investment groups developing Hindu guidelines for ethical investment. This helps Hindus use their money in ways that do not conflict with beliefs such as vegetarianism.

CONTINUING THE LIFE CYCLE

Swami Vibudhesha Teertha, Acharya (guru or spiritual master) of Madhvacarya Vaishnavas, has written the following:

Hindu religion wants its followers to live a simple life. It does not allow people to go on increasing their material wants. People are meant to learn to enjoy spiritual happiness, so that to derive a sense of satisfaction and fulfillment, they need not run after material pleasures and disturb nature's checks and balances. They have to milk a cow and enjoy, not cut at the udder of the cow with greed to enjoy what is not available in the natural course. Do not use anything belonging to nature, such as oil, coal, or forest, at a greater rate than you can replenish it. For example, do not destroy birds, fish, earthworms, and even bacteria which play vital ecological roles; once they are annihilated you cannot recreate them. Thus only can you avoid becoming bankrupt, and the life cycle can continue for a long, long time.

(Hindu Faith Statement, www.arcworld.org)

CONVERSION

The spiritual power of Hinduism and its teacher-saints has drawn many people toward this religion. In the 20th and 21st centuries people from around the world have pursued Hindu wisdom and some have converted to Hinduism. Conversions have happened despite the fact that traditionally a non-Hindu cannot convert to Hinduism. Hindus believed that one could only be a Hindu if one was born into a Hindu household.

With some notable exceptions it has only been possible to convert to Hinduism since the end of the 19th century. It was Christianity, with its missionary spirit and its idea of conversion, that influenced many Hindu reform movements. One way a non-Hindu could convert to Hinduism is by following the Hindu dharma and samsara very diligently. The convert could celebrate various Hindu ceremonies and rituals, become the student of a guru, change his or her name, and thus work at becoming a Hindu. Eventually, within a generation or two, through marriage and other social interactions, one could call oneself a Hindu.

This option for conversion is similar to the way in which a lower-caste family can now rise to a higher caste. Traditionally a non-Hindu or lower-caste family could not even interact with a Hindu family of a higher status. Recently, though, it has become possible for a low-caste family to ascend gradually to a higher caste. To do so the family adopts the rituals, religious ceremonies, and general way of living of a higher-caste family. In addition such an ascent is made more achievable by taking up vegetarianism, marrying into a higher caste, or both.

TRANSCENDENTAL MEDITATION

In its early days Transcendental Meditation, a meditation technique introduced by the Maharishi Mahesh Yogi, attracted the British pop groups the Beatles and the Rolling Stones and the American actress Mia Farrow as devotees. Although its claims have been challenged by many, Transcendental Meditation has attracted to its fold more than 6 million people from all walks of life and educational backgrounds. It does not necessarily lead people to become Hindu converts, but it does lead to the practice of some of its spiritualizing techniques. Maharishi Mahesh Yogi died in February 2008.

AMERICAN MOVEMENTS IN HINDUISM

These modern adjustments to the Hindu caste system and its new openness to accepting converts have had significant effects on the establishment of Hinduism in North America during the last half-century. Many individuals from the West who are attracted to Hinduism feel spiritually empty in a secular world that puts emphasis upon material belongings and within Hinduism they find a rewarding spiritual path and way of life.

MAHARISHI MAHESH YOGI

The early responses to Hindu spirituality in America often were reactions to the calls of particular teacher-saints rather than entries into the full richness of Hinduism. Maharishi Mahesh Yogi, after spending two years in retreat in the foothills of the Himalayas, began as a guru in 1957 teaching a basic meditation technique that he later called Transcendental Meditation. This program, which Maharishi Mahesh Yogi introduced to the West, attempts in its simple technique under the guidance of a certified teacher to help practitioners gain deep relaxation, eliminate stress, promote health, increase creativity and intelligence, and attain inner happiness and fulfillment.

INTERNATIONAL SOCIETY FOR KRISHNA CONSCIOUSNESS

Almost at the same time another Hindu saint-teacher, Srila Prabhupada, came to the United States to initiate a more devotional Hindu movement in the West. In 1965 he started the International Society for Krishna Consciousness. He had followed the four stages of life traditional in Hinduism, beginning as a young man studying the Vedic scriptures, taking on the responsibilities of married life, and at the age of 54 retiring to the life of a forest dweller to devote more time to study and writing.

At the age of 63 he became a *sanyasin* (ascetic), writing over 40 volumes of translation and commentary on the Bhagavad Gita, Bhagavata Purana, and other Hindu classics, and living a life of devotion to God by meditation and chanting. His best-known personal title was Bhaktivedanta, a compound of *bhakti* (devotion) and *Vedanta* (deep understanding of the goal of spiritual knowledge). He gathered hundreds of followers in the United States, called the Hare Krishna movement. His mission has continued and has spread to more than 50

HARE KRISHNA

During the early days of the Krishna Consciousness movement, gatherings of Hare Krishna devotees were often seen in railroad stations, bus terminals, and airports dressed in their robes, chanting their mantra:

Hare Krishna, Hare Krishna, Krishna, Krishna, Hare, Hare Hare Rama, Hare Rama, Rama, Rama, Hare, Hare

This chant called listeners and the chanters themselves to Krishna (the all-attractive Supreme Being) and Rama (the highest eternal pleasure), inviting by its sounds all people to become aware that the Supreme Being is the source of all things, thereby inviting them to Krishna consciousness.

centers in the United States and Canada and has extended itself to many countries throughout the world.

Mahesh Yogi and Bhaktivedanta were both gurus, or saint-teachers, whose spiritual power marked them as Hindu guides or

Krishna devotees chanting and dancing in praise of Krishna along a city street in Medellin, Columbia.

leaders. Each had many followers or disciples. They provided one avenue toward a greater understanding of Hinduism in America. However there are other paths to Hinduism.

KNOWLEDGE OF HINDUISM

Many individuals interested in Hinduism visit local Hindu temples, explore the faith through academic courses, or visit study centers established in the United States. Such studies lead some of them to participate in prayer and chant sessions. Although they may not be devotees of Hinduism they are continually gaining in their appreciation of the Hindu religion.

There are also centers with classes in comparative religions that attempt to familiarize people with the beliefs and practices of various religions, including Hinduism. Thus knowledge of various aspects of Hinduism certainly has grown in America over the last four decades. For example the practice of yoga as a form of meditation and health regime is now very popular and is as likely to be held in a Catholic church hall as it is in a Hindu temple. For many the specifically "Hindu" aspects of such a tradition are not as significant as the practice of techniques to calm the mind and body.

HINDU TEMPLES IN AMERICA

Hinduism, an open and vital religion, has also adapted itself well to the nature of American culture and an environment that is becoming more and more diverse and open to understanding. Today there are more than 200 Hindu temples and ashrams in the United States and three-quarters of them have been built since 1975. There are such centers in almost every part of the country, in every state and in every major metropolitan area. Many of these temples are converted from former church buildings. Others have been built from scratch, often following all the traditional Hindu architectural guidelines for the construction of a temple or a sacred space. These temples are worlds in themselves that offer a haven for a minority community to live and act out its identity.

LIFE AT PENN HILLS TEMPLE

The temple at Penn Hills in Pittsburgh, Pennsylvania, is characteristic of the newer Hindu temples in the United States. Consecrated in 1976, the temple is one of the earliest built in North America. Many additions, alterations, and modifications have been made to the traditional architectural plan in order for it to suit modern devotees living in a technological society. Many of the ritual practices of the temple have been adapted as well. Although *puja* is held each day, major rituals are held on the weekends for the convenience of busy patrons. Certain regulations and rules observed in traditional Hindu temples have been omitted here. For one thing the temple has a parking lot just outside its premises because the modern devotee has neither time nor energy to climb hills to visit the temple. Although in many Hindu temples non-Hindus are not allowed near the innermost sanctuary, at Penn Hills regular weekend tours are organized for non-Hindus. These tours aim to make visitors understand the rich meaning of the Hindu temple, its icons, and its religious rituals. A kitchen, a restaurant, and restrooms have also been incorporated into the temple complex.

In 1996 the Hindu Temple of Atlanta, in Riverdale, Georgia, completed its building work using traditional Indian architectural forms and skills and has become an attraction for many visitors who simply want to experience the style of Indian temples. More than 2,000 hand-carved stone figurines were shipped from India to dress the facade. The temple regularly hosts a congregation of more than 500.

One of the most impressive temples, built by members of the Bochasanwasi Shri Akshar Purushottam Swaminarayan Sanstha (BAPS) in 2004, is the Shri Swaminarayan Mandir in Stafford, Texas. It serves the Hindu community of Greater Houston and is the first all-stone *mandira* built in the United States. It is a stunning work of Hindu architecture that has also become a main tourist attraction in the Houston area.

ANCIENT VALUES, NEW IDEAS

The history of Hinduism shows over and over the diverse and original ideas and beliefs of this religion. Though Hinduism is rooted in ancient values and beliefs, it is constantly incorporating new ideas. This change is evident in spiritual yogic movements brought to the West by the living saints, in the architectural innovations in the traditional temple plan, in the possibility of conversion to Hinduism by non-Hindus, and even the ascension of the hierarchical ladder or caste system.

Hinduism keeps itself rooted in its traditions, but its adherents introduce innovations through reform movements when the

Opened in 2004, the Shri Swaminarayan Temple in Bartlett, Illinois, has been built using traditional Hindu architectural styles and craftsmanship. There are more than 200 Hindu temples and hundreds of Hindu centers throughout the United States.

time requires it. Not only are many Hindu traditions, such as the low status of women and low castes changing in the country of its origin, but this ancient religion is also making modifications for its expatriated devotees.

FACT FILE

Worldwide Numbers
The Hindu faith has more than 950 million followers. Almost all of them live in southeast Asia.

Holy Symbol
This is the written form of the sacred sound "Aum," which Hindus believe to be the first sound from which the rest of the universe was created.

Holy Writings
There are many sacred texts. Among them are the Vedas, which highlight how religious life should be conducted. The Upanishads are hymns and poems that ask about life, creation, love, and suffering. They are mostly written in the ancient Indian language Sanskrit.

Holy Places
Among the most important are the Himalayas and the river Ganges, especially where it flows through the city of Varanasi (Benares).

Founders
There is not a single founder but thousands of gurus who draw upon different teachings. A guru is named as someone who has obtained wisdom through practice and knowledge.

Festivals
There are many major festivals throughout the year including Mahashivaratri, a festival devoted to the deity Shiva (February); Holi, the festival of fertility and harvest (February/ March); and Divali, the festival of lights. Divali extends over a period of five days and is seen as important because it emphasizes good's triumph over evil (celebrated in October/ November).

BIBLIOGRAPHY

Clément, Catherine. *Gandhi, the power of pacifism.* Discoveries. New York: H.N. Abrams, 1996.

Jansen, Eva Rudy. *The Book of Hindu Imagery: Gods, Manifestations, and Their Meaning.* York Beach, Me.: Samuel Weiser, 1993.

Mahony, William K. *The Artful Universe: An Introduction to the Vedic Religious Imagination.* Albany: State University of New York Press, 1998.

O'Flaherty, Wendy Doniger. *Hindu Myths.* Harmondsworth, U.K.: Penguin Books, 1975.

"Hindu Faith Statement." Alliance for Religions and Conservation. Available online. URL: www.arcworld.org. Accessed November 6, 2008.

FOR FURTHER READING

Breuilly, Elizabeth, and O'Brien Joanne, and Palmer, Martin. *Religions of the World.* New York: Checkmark Books, 2005.

Editors of *Hinduism Today Magazine. What is Hinduism?* Kapaa, Hawaii: Himalayan Academy, 2007.

Klostermaier, Klaus K. *A Survey of Hinduism.* Albany: State University of New York Press, 2007.

Knott, Kim. *Hinduism: A Very Short Introduction.* Oxford: Oxford University Press, 2000.

Michaels, Axel. *Hinduism: Past and Present.* Princeton, N.J.: Princeton University Press, 2004.

Mookerjee, Ajit. *Ritual Art of India.* Rochester, Vt.: Inner Traditions, 1998.

O'Brien, Joanne, Martin Palmer, David B. Barrett, and Joanne O'Brien. *The Atlas of Religion.* Berkeley: University of California Press, 2007.

Rinehart, Robin, ed. *Contemporary Hinduism: Ritual, Culture, and Practice.* Santa Barbara, Calif.: ABC-Clio, 2004.

Rosen, Steven. *Essential Hinduism.* Westport, Conn.: Praeger, 2007.

Shah, Bharat S. Sanskrit: *An Appreciation Without Apprehension.* Charleston, S.C.: BookSurge Publishing, 2005.

Sharma, Arvind. *The Study of Hinduism.* Studies in Comparative Religion. Columbia, S.C.: University of South Carolina Press, 2003.

Shattuck, Cybelle T. *Hinduism.* Upper Saddle River, N.J.: Prentice Hall, 1999.

Strohmeier, John, ed. *The Bhagavad Gita according to Gandhi.* Berkeley, Calif.: Berkeley Hills Books, 2000.

Viswanathan, Ed. *Am I a Hindu? The Hinduism Primer.* Glen Ellen, Calif.: Halo Books, 1992.

WEB SITES

Further facts and figures, history, and current status of the religion can be found on the following Web sites:

www.hinduwebsite.com
Resources and comprehensive information on beliefs, traditions, history, scriptures, philosophy, practices, scriptures, and symbolism of Hinduism.

www.bbc.co.uk/religion/religions/hinduism
A guide to Hinduism, including gods and beliefs, festivals, everyday life, and rituals.

www.religioustolerance.org
An overview and summaries on chief deities, sacred texts, beliefs, and the caste system.

GLOSSARY

Agni—"Fire." The term also refers to the Vedic god of fire, Agni, who is the archetypal priest.

ashrama—A forest retreat where sages, ascetics, religious teachers, and their students live. Also the term for the four stages of life.

atman—The soul of an individual. The term refers to the essence within people, which is identical to the essence of the Universal Power considered as the source of everything.

avatar—An incarnation of god who descends to earth in human form to save humankind from calamities.

Bhagavad Gita—A sixth book of the epic Mahabharata in which the god Krishna teaches Arjuna about self-duty and devotion.

bhakti—Devotion, faith, and love. Most often expressed by a complete devotion to a personal god.

Brahma—The creator god, also known as Prajapati. One of the gods of the triad formed by Vishnu, Shiva, and Brahma. His consort is Sarasvati, the goddess of knowledge.

Brahman—The One God of Hinduism, also known as the One, the Ultimate Reality, and the World Soul. He is the self-existing Universal Power, which is believed to be the source of everything.

Brahmanas—Ritual texts attached to the four Vedas.

Brahmin—The uppermost class of the Hindu caste system, whose duties are to perform rituals and to teach.

brahmachari—The student. This is the first of the four stages of life.

darsana—Sacred "seeing" of a deity by a devotee.

devas—A class of Vedic gods.

dharma—Social duty or religious law. The principle of order in Hindu society and ultimately in the universe.

grihasthin—The householder. This is the second of four stages of Hindu life.

guru—A spiritual teacher who is considered to be a divine manifestation.

jivanmukta—People who have attained spiritual liberation while still alive; those who are in a state of perfection and have realized unity with Brahman.

karma—Good and bad deeds or acts in a person's previous or present life that will determine the quality of the next incarnation.

Kshatriya—The second highest caste, the warriors, whose duty is to fight and defend.

lingam—Phallus. The male generative organ that symbolizes Shiva's erotic power as well as his ascetic power.

mandira **or** *mandir*—The Hindu temple.

mantra—A sacred formula, syllable, or utterance, usually a ritual statement or verse prayer.

maya—The illusion one has that this transitory world is permanent while living in it.

moksha—Enlightenment; release.

mudras—Symbolic hand gestures, the origin of which lies in Indian classical dance. They are also extensively used in creating sacred images.

murtis—The artistic representations of Hindu deities, which, after ritual consecration, become the focus of worship.

polytheism—The belief in many gods.

prasada—In a theological context it signifies the grace of God whereby one is liberated from the cycle of rebirth. In a devotional context it refers to the food blessed by the gods and returned to the devotees. It also signifies the temple as the seat or hub of religious life.

puja—Worship in which a deity is honored by the offerings of flowers, incense, food, and other everyday items.

pujari—A worshipper; a Brahmin priest who performs the puja.

rishis—Sages who had perceived the Ultimate Reality and who revealed the texts of the Upanishads.

rita—The Vedic term for the cosmic and ethical order of things, the later extension of which is the concept of dharma.

samsara—The cycles of a soul's birth and rebirth through difficult lifetimes. Reincarnation.

samskara—Rites of passage.

Shaiva—The name of the cult of Shiva and his followers.

Shakta—The name for the cult of Mahadevi Shakti and her followers.

Shakti—The Great Goddess of energy and power.

Untouchable – the name given to the group of people who performed the most menial tasks in society. They are now called Dalit (downtrodden) and officially known as 'scheduled castes'.

vahana—"Vehicle." The term used to describe a god's means of transportation.

varnasramadharma—The Hindu system of social responsibilities as one passes through the various stages of life: as a student of the Veda, the father of a family, a retired man searching for life's meaning, and an ascetic pursuing liberation from rebirth.

Veda—Earliest Hindu texts, composed before, during, and after the Aryan invasion of the Indus Valley.

INDEX

Mahabharata War, the 64–65
Mahadevi Shakti 67–69
mandira 15, 92–100, 106–107, 109, 135–136
marriage *(vivah)* 125–126
Maruts, the 27
meditation 37, 38; Transcendental Meditation 132, 133
moksha 12, 14, 15, 16, 17, 41, 42–43, 101, 114
mountains, sacred 95, 96
Mughal Empire 78–79
munis (silent ones) 37
murti (sacred statues) 102–104, 105

N
Nehru, Jawaharlal (1889–1964) 86
Nepal, Hinduism in 8, 90

P
partition of India 85–86
Parvati 48, 49, 52, 53, 54, 67, 68
pilgrimage centers *(tirtha sthana)* 94, 100–102
poetry 71–72, 78, 83
priests *See* Brahmins
puja (daily worship) 14, 15, 104–109
puranas 14, 45, 50, 70–72, 94
purity 20, 37

R
raksasas (demons) 49, 54, 56, 57, 62, 64, 69
Rama 14, 58
Ramakrishna (1836–1886) 82–83
Ramanuja (1017–1137) 73–74
Ramayana, the 14, 45, 58, 62
Rashtriya Swayamsevak Sangh (RSS) **88–89**
Ravana, King 58–61
reincarnation (samsara) 12, 14, 41–42, 113–114

rishis (having the power of knowledge) 11, 37
rituals and rites of passage 12, 14, 16–17, 34–38; childhood rituals 121–124; death 16–17, 81, 82, 126–127; dharma (religious duties) 14, 16; *griha* 31; icons *(murti)* 103; in the *mandira* 98–99; marriage *(vivah)* 125–126; prenatal rituals 121; *puja* (daily worship) 14, 15, 104–109; purity 20; sacrifices 12, 31–34, 39–40
Roy, Rammohan (1772–1833) 81–82
Rudra 27, 46–47

S
sacrifices 12, 31–34, 39–40
saints in Hinduism 128–130
samsara (reincarnation) 12, 14, 41–42, 113–114
sanyasin (the ascetic) 119–120
satyagraha 85, 86, 88
scriptures 11–15, 17, 62, 112, 113; Bhagavad Gita 13–14, 17, 56, 65–66, 67, 73, 74, 116; *puranas* 14, 45, 50, 70–72, 94; the Upanishads 11–12, 38–40, 42, 43–44; the Vedas 11–12, 18–20, 24–26, 32, 33, 34–36, 73–74, 115–116
separatist movements 90
Shaivism 15, 48, 50
Shiva 22, 27, 46–50, 51, 52, 53, 54–56, 59
shrauta rituals 31, 32
shruti 11–12, 38–39, 45, 112
Sita 59–60, 61–62
Skanda (Kartikeya) 48, 51, 53–56
smriti 11, 13–14, 112
suttee 81, 82

T
Tagore, Rabindranath (1861–1941) 83–84, 85
tapas (heat of knowledge) 37, 40
Teertha, Swami Vibudhesha 131
temples 15, 92–100, 106–107, 109, 135–136
10 avatars, the 56–58, 58–67
tirtha sthana (pilgrimage centers) 94, 100–102
Transcendental Meditation 132, 133

U
Ultimate Reality, the *See* Brahman
United States, Hinduism in 132–136
upanayana ritual 123–124
Upanishadic period 38–45, 113
Upanishads, the 11–12, 38–40, 42, 43–44

V
Vaishnavism 15, 56
Vaishyas 117
vanaprasthin (the forest dweller) 119
varnas 115–120
varnasramadharma 114–115
Vayu 27, 59
Vedanta Sutras 73–74
Vedas, the 11–12, 18–20, 24–26, 32, 33, 34–36, 73–74, 115–116
Vedic period, the 24–38, 113
Vishnu 14, 26, 51, 55, 56–67
Vishwa Hindu Parishad (VHP) 89

W
women, in Hinduism 71, 81

Y
yoga 43, 53, 130

ABOUT THE AUTHOR

Madhu Bazaz Wangu has taught at the University of Pittsburgh, where she earned a Ph.D. in religious studies. She is the winner of several awards for her work as a freelance artist and has also taught classes in the Hindi language.

ABOUT THE SERIES EDITORS

Martin Palmer is the founder of ICOREC (International Consultancy on Religion, Education, and Culture) in 1983 and is the secretary-general of the Alliance of Religions and Conservation (ARC). He is the author of many books on world religions.

Joanne O'Brien has an M.A. degree in theology and has written a range of educational and general reference books on religion and contemporary culture. She is co-author, with Martin Palmer and Elizabeth Breuilly, of *Religions of the World* and *Festivals of the World* published by Facts On File Inc.

PICTURE CREDITS